The Pocket Guide to
UNDERWATER DIVING

Reg Vallintine

Bell & Hyman

The Pocket Guide to Underwater Diving
was designed and edited by
Holland & Clark Limited, London

Designer
Julian Holland

Editors
Philip Clark
Christine McMullen

Artist
Martin Smillie

Published by Bell & Hyman
Denmark House, 37/39 Queen Elizabeth Street,
London SE1 2QB

British Library Cataloguing in Publication Data
Vallintine, Reg
    The pocket guide to underwater diving.
    1. Swimming   2. Diving
    I. Title
    797.2   GV837
ISBN 0-7135-2510-X

Phototypeset in Great Britain by
Tradespools Limited, Frome, Somerset

Printed and bound in Great Britain by
Purnell & Sons Limited, Paulton

Acknowledgements
The author would like to thank Mike Holbrook,
BSAC National Diving Officer, and Dr Peter
Wilmshurst of the National Medical Committee for
reading and commenting on the text. The help of
the BSAC Lecture Notes compiled by Jerry Hazzard
and permission to use the BritishSub-Aqua Club Air
Diving Decompression Tables is also gratefully
acknowledged.

Photo Credits
Cover picture by Mike Portelly
All other photography by Paul Arbiter

Contents

Introduction

Diving is fun. It can be enjoyed by everyone, old or young, providing they are moderately fit. All too often however, potential divers are put off by the imagined dangers and technical complications.

This book is designed to give you, in the simplest possible way, the elementary knowledge that will enable you to dive safely. It will not replace qualified instruction on a dive course. Neither will it help you to qualify for high awards, but it will act as a guide and an 'aide-memoire' to basic training.

You will have a great time – providing you follow the rules and don't take risks. Remember that the best diver is not the one who goes deepest, but the one who comes back every time! Good divers arrive alive!

You don't need to be a champion swimmer to take up the sport, but you do need a competent and qualified instructor. The appendices at the end of the book give some clues on where to find one.

Before that we will look at the most common equipment, the principal hazards and how these can be overcome by common sense and by following the rules of diving.

Experience should be built up gradually, don't rush or be pushed into diving when or where you don't feel confident. The book will also give you a good idea of what to expect on your first open water dive.

More and more people are diving and enjoying it. You don't know what you are missing unless you give it a try. Start today and many happy returns to the surface!

History of Diving

How Diving Developed

People have been diving for thousands of years since primitive man first ducked underwater to search for shellfish as food.

The first underwater divers just held their breath while swimming down to gather oysters and even coral from considerable depths.

The most famous divers of antiquity were Scyllias, the Greek, and his daughter, Cyana. Scyllias was employed by the King of Persia to bring up sunken treasure, but the king refused to let Scyllias return to his homeland. Eventually Scyllias avenged himself by teaching Cyana to dive with a breathing tube and then, together, they swam down in a storm and cast off the anchors of the Persian fleet causing a great disaster.

Today Japanese 'Amas', girl divers, still continue Cyana's tradition by gathering oysters, shellfish and edible seaweed wearing only goggles.

Another famous ancient diver was an Egyptian, Issa, who served with the fleets of Saladin. The Crusaders had blockaded the city of Acre, but Issa managed to smuggle money and letters ashore using a form of breathing tube and helmet which allowed him to swim just below the surface.

In more recent centuries there have been many developments in the equipment men have used to assist them in diving. A large number of these inventions would not have worked because of the increase in water pressure on the body as depth is gained. In fact, it is impossible to breathe surface air

Above: The diver depicted in this anonymous manuscript of 1430 has a tube to the surface supported by floats. He would be unable to breathe except at very shallow depths unless air was pumped down to him.

down a simple pipe at a depth of more than 45 cm (18 ins) because the increasing pressure on the chest muscles prevents them functioning. This is one reason why snorkel tubes are short and why the intrepid explorer in the drawing (above) would have had problems!

The First Diving Bells

The earliest really successful diving devices were 'bells'. The diving bell in its simplest form is merely a large container which has been up-ended and weighted to sink with its occup-

ant until it is just off the sea bed. The underwater worker can then breathe the air trapped in the bell while searching or working below the level of the water in the bell. Soon, however, the carbon dioxide (CO_2) from his exhaled breath would make the mixture in the bell unbreathable.

Halley's Bell

To overcome this problem, the British scientist and astronomer, Halley, developed an improved bell which allowed for barrels of fresh air to be sent down and up-ended under the bell to re-purify the air. His workers

Above: Dr Edmund Halley, the astronomer, after whom Halley's Comet was named, produced his diving bell in 1690.

Weights at the bottom kept it down and a plate of glass on the top let in light. A hole in the lid of the lead-lined air barrel is connected to a weighted leather tube which hung down as it was lowered. The 'bell man' caught the tube and raised it into the bell, causing the fresh air to run in.

Halley, who used the bell himself, reported that he and four others had stayed successfully at a depth of 54 feet (16.6 metres) for as long as one and a half hours.

working underwater.

One successful apparatus was designed and produced in 1715 by John Lethbridge, a Devon man. His 'tube' was filled with fresh air from bellows on the surface and he was lowered into the sea with his bare arms projecting from it. The apparatus became difficult to use at a depth of 20 metres (66 feet) due to the pressure on his arms, as the rest of his body was kept at close to normal atmospheric pressure. Nevertheless, Lethbridge operated successfully for many years, recovering precious items from wrecks for the Dutch East India Company.

Helmet Apparatus

Many other experiments culminated in the very successful helmet diving apparatus which became the standard gear for working divers during the last century and for the first half of this. Evolving from an original design by John Deane of Whitstable, the air was pumped down to the diver from the surface. His body was therefore maintained at the pressure of the surrounding water as he breathed the compressed air.

The diver was heavily weighted and lowered by a lifeline to the bottom where he walked slowly on lead-soled boots to his place of work on the sea bed.

John Deane worked on the wrecks of the *Mary Rose* and the *Royal George* in the Solent.

Sport Diving

The idea of diving as a sport evolved only during the last 50 years or so. In 1878, two Frenchmen, Rouquayrol

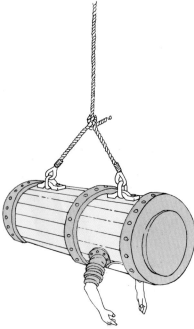

Above: John Lethbridge in his wooden 'diving engine'. It was six feet (1.8 metres) long and 2½ feet (80 cm) wide. It had a four-inch (10 cm) window which he looked through as he lay on his front, using hands and arms to work.

also left the bell for short periods while underwater, breathing air from tubes leading from the main supply.

Successful Designs

Many sorts of diving apparatus were developed and built by inventors. A large number did not survive because little was known about the laws which govern breathing and

and Denayrouze, produced light-weight diving equipment which could be used independently of the surface by means of a small container of compressed air.

The major development, however, was the provision of a 'demand regulator' which allowed the diver to breathe his air at the same pressure as the surrounding water.

Diving Clubs
These developments led to the first diving clubs in which members walked round on the bottom of tanks with cylinders of air clutched to their chests!

During the Second World War the exploits of 'frogmen' using oxygen apparatus publicised the advantages of flippers or fins, which allowed divers to swim over the bottom in the manner of fish.

Cousteau's Aqualung
Jacques Cousteau, an officer in the French Navy, together with the engineer, Emile Gagnon, produced an 'aqualung' with a fully automatic demand valve or regulator which could supply air at the right pressure on demand.

After the war, the aqualung was exported and developed in many countries and 'Scuba Diving' became the fastest growing sport in America.

In Britain, the British Sub-Aqua Club became the governing body of the sport and banded divers together in branches throughout the country.

The age of the aqualung had arrived!

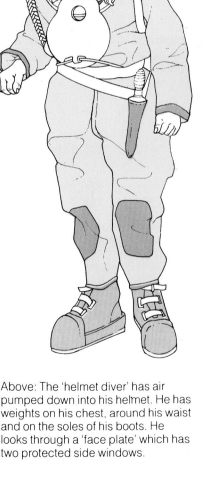

Above: The 'helmet diver' has air pumped down into his helmet. He has weights on his chest, around his waist and on the soles of his boots. He looks through a 'face plate' which has two protected side windows.

Training and Opportunities

BSAC

Although modern sport diving apparatus is extremely reliable, it is vital that a diver learns the techniques necessary from a qualified instructor or through a well-established diving club. The British Sub-Aqua Club (BSAC) was founded in 1953 and now has over 1,000 branches in 30 countries.

Branch members become individual members of the BSAC as a whole and for their subscription they receive a copy of the Club's comprehensive *Diving Manual* and the magazine *Diver*.

Diving School

During recent years, many of those who are anxious to complete a comprehensive training in the shortest possible time have learnt through diving schools. Those schools with nationally qualified instructors are recognised by the BSAC.

The Undersea World

Diving is not merely a healthy activity but provides a unique opportunity to explore. It is a world in which it is still possible to make discoveries – wrecks draw the adventurous diver and divers may develop interest in underwater archaeology, photography or film-making.

Right: This fortunate beginner is learning in the Red Sea, one of the most beautiful diving areas in the world. The instructor is adjusting her equipment before they leave the surface. She is wearing a combination lifejacket and aqualung harness.

Part 1 Equipment

Basic Equipment

The basic equipment of a diver consists of a face mask, snorkel tube and a pair of flippers or fins. 'Snorkel diving' with this equipment alone, provides a fascinating sport in its own right, especially in seas that are clear and warm.

Basic equipment is also essential for aqualung divers, and to this is added compressed air-breathing apparatus to allow a longer time underwater.

The Mask

The mask allows you to see clearly underwater. The human eye is designed to see in air and vision becomes distorted when the eye is immersed in water. Put an air space between the eye and the water, however, and you can see clearly again.

Because of the refraction of light through the glass of the mask, objects tend to look larger and closer than they really are. After a few dives you will adjust mentally to this.

Fitting the Mask

The mask should cover the eyes and nose of the diver and should have two pockets at the side of the nose so that the nose can be held by the fingers from outside the mask. It should also have an adjustable strap which allows the sides of the mask to be held firmly against the face.

When buying or choosing a mask it is useful to see if you can hold it against you face without the use of the strap by breathing in gently through the nose. Look down, and if the mask does not drop off while you

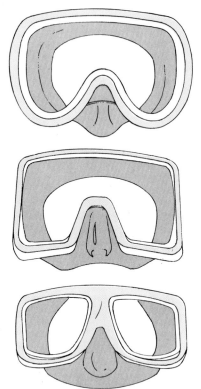

Above: The field of vision from a face mask depends on the size of the glass and on how close it is to the face. Smaller masks are better for snorkelling as they have less air volume to adjust if they squeeze. Aqualung divers need a comfortable mask that fits the face and does not leak. Try several on before making a final choice. Modern masks made of translucent 'silicone' rubber let in more light and allow movement to be seen through the sides. They are more expensive but, on the other hand, they should last longer.

are holding your breath, then it is a reasonable fit and should not leak.

Before wearing the mask it is advisable to take action to stop it misting up inside when you go underwater. Various preparations exist to prevent condensation but the simplest and traditional way is to spit into the mask, rub the spittle well into the glass and then rinse it out in the water.

When you wear the mask make sure that you do not have any of your hair inside as this will allow water to seep in.

The Snorkel Tube

The snorkel tube is designed to allow you to breathe the surface air while looking down into the water.

The snorkel should consist of a simple 'J' or 'L' shaped tube with a mouthpiece. The two nodules of the mouthpiece are designed to be held gently between the teeth and the guard fits between the lips and gums. The diver breathes gently in and out through his mouth.

The tube is fixed upright by attaching it to the mask strap or slipping it between the strap and the diver's head. Avoid snorkel tubes that have valves of various kinds as these have a tendency to leak.

Fins

Fins provide the diver with an efficient means of propulsion, leaving the hands and arms free for other purposes. There are two main types available: those into which the whole foot can be pushed and be fully protected and those which feature an adjustable heel strap.

Above: The best snorkel tubes are made of heavy duty rubber that will fit comfortable against the diver's head or leg. Alternatively snorkels can be hung around the neck using a cord. The top end is often wound with luminous tape so that the snorkeller can be seen and distinguished from a seal or other sea creature.

There are many shapes and sizes, but in rougher seas a slightly longer tube may help the beginner.

In any case, if water does come in you need to become accustomed to blowing it out before inhaling air.

The former tend to be easier to operate in the early stages of training but the adjustable fin has the advantage later on, in that it may still be used when wetsuit bootees are worn on the feet.

Finning Technique

If you have never used a mask, tube and fins before it is best to begin by becoming accustomed to the fins alone.

Put your fins on and then lie on your back in the shallow end and beat your legs slowly up and down in a 'crawl' kick so that the fin surfaces push against the water. This will move you along quite rapidly.

Then roll over on to your front and continue. While swimming on your front you will need to lean backwards from the waist occasionally to allow you to take a breath. Try to avoid bending the knees and splashing on the surface when 'finning'. The movements should come from the hips with only a little play at the knees and ankles.

Once you can move comfortably using the fins you can try fitting the mask. Now you will be able to see the bottom as you swim along.

Finally, add the snorkel tube

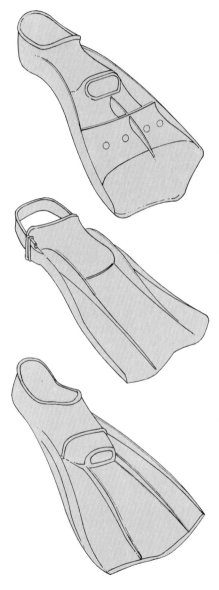

Right: Fins come in different shapes and sizes. The fin in the centre can be adjusted for use either with or without bootees. Your instructor or local dive shop will give you advice on which fins should be most suitable for you. Very small fins may be easy to use in a pool but it will mean that you have to work extremely hard to move along under the sea.

which will make it possible for you to breathe without having to lift your head.

Now try moving very gently along the surface. Imagine that you are watching fish on the bottom, and remember that they will be disturbed if you splash.

The Duck Dive

When you feel happy on the surface try a duck dive. Start by lying flat and stationary on the top of the water in a depth of two metres or so. When you are ready, take a deep breath through the snorkel and hold it.

Then bend vertically downwards from the waist, flip your fins out of the water and glide to the bottom. Once your fins are underwater, beat them gently to maintain your momentum. Swim along the bottom for a few seconds and then gently return to the surface.

Blow out sharply through the snorkel tube to push out the water that came in when you dived, and carry on swimming and breathing on the surface.

During snorkelling you are, of course, breathing through the mouth alone. When you get back to the shallows, stand on the bottom in waist-high water, remove your mask but hold your snorkel in place, and lean forward so that your head is in the water. Now practise breathing through the snorkel while your nose is in contact with the water. This can be difficult to learn but persevere until you find you can breathe easily.

The Aqualung

The compressed air breathing apparatus used by sports divers is called an aqualung in Britain and SCUBA (self-contained underwater breathing apparatus) in the United States of America.

It has three main parts, the *cylinder* or *bottle* ('tank' in the USA), the *harness* ('backpak' in the USA) and the *demand valve* ('regulator'), which reduces the pressure of air you breathe from the cylinder.

Below: The snorkeller swims slowly along, breathing through his snorkel. He propels himself forwards by pushing each fin downwards in turn.

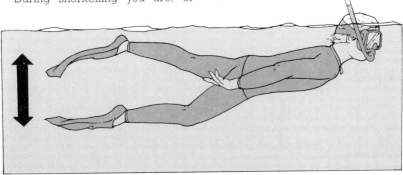

Breathing High Pressure Air

The air is pumped into the cylinder through a compressor especially designed to produce high pressure breathing air (currently 200 atmospheres or 'bars'). It incorporates at least two filters. The first filter usually contains silica gel to remove water vapour and the second has activated carbon to remove most other impurities that may be found in air. Although people breathe in some pollution from the atmosphere in the normal course of events, the impurities are greatly concentrated in pressurised air. Therefore the risk of being poisoned would be enormously increased if good filters were not fitted.

The Cylinder

The air from the compressor is pumped into the cylinder via a 'pillar valve' at the top end and a seal is provided by a rubber 'O' ring. The cylinder is turned on and off by a tap, either at the side of the pillar valve or at the top. Some cylinders have an automatic reserve system – a lever which can be pulled down with a rigid wire and loop fixed on the side of the cylinder. If this form of reserve is to be used, make sure that the reserve lever is in the 'up'

Fitting the Demand Valve

The first stage of the demand valve is fixed on to the cylinder pillar valve by removing the dust cap and fitting the air entry port into the circular groove which contains the 'O' ring. The locking screw at the other end of the demand valve 'A' clamp is then screwed up into the indentation on the rear of the pillar valve. The screw should be tightened firmly but not forcefully, as the compressed air will form its own seal. Check that the second stage is the right way up for breathing with the mouthpiece above the exhaust ports.

Screw to fix to cylinder

Mouthpiece

Connecting pressure tube

'A' clamp

Dust cap

Exhaust ports

Purge valve

Demand valve second stage

Demand valve first stage

The aqualung completely
assembled looks complicated but is
simple to operate. It fits on the diver's
back. He breathes through the
mouthpiece just as he does with a
snorkel tube.

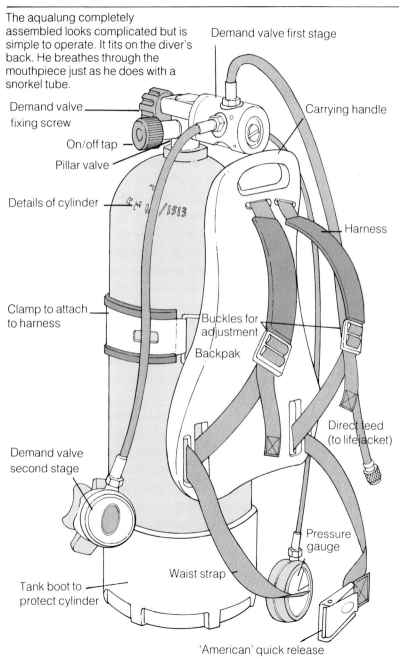

Demand valve first stage

Carrying handle

Demand valve
fixing screw

On/off tap

Pillar valve

Details of cylinder

Harness

Clamp to attach
to harness

Buckles for
adjustment

Backpak

Demand valve
second stage

Direct feed
(to lifejacket)

Pressure
gauge

Waist strap

Tank boot to
protect cylinder

'American' quick release

position before entering the water.

If the pressure falls towards the end of the dive, a valve inside the cylinder makes it noticeably harder to breathe and thereby warns the diver that it is time to 'pull the reserve' to release more air for the return to the surface.

The Demand Valve

The demand valve or regulator has two main 'stages'. The first stage, which fixes on to the cylinder, automatically reduces the air pressure to around 10 bars above the water pressure surrounding it. This air then travels down a tube to the second stage which includes the mouthpiece through which the diver breathes. Inside the second stage is a diaphragm in contact with the water on one side and an air space on the other. The air space is designed to refill after each breath taken.

What happens is that as the diver breathes in, the pressure drops in the air space and the diaphragm bends towards the mouth, thus triggering a lever which allows air to enter the chamber until the diaphragm is straightened by the air pressure on the inside. Each mouthful of air is thus supplied at exactly the pressure of the surrounding water.

This is one of the most important principles of the aqualung. The air is provided on demand at the surrounding pressure which prevents the lungs being squeezed. However, it is also potentially dangerous if used incorrectly (see page 45).

The demand valve is usually fitted with a lead to a pressure gauge which shows the amount of air left in the cylinder. When the needle drops into the red or shaded area at the bottom of the dial, it is obviously time to start to ascend to the surface.

Fitting the Aqualung

A harness attaches the cylinder to the diver's back and can be adjusted so that the cylinder sits comfortably.

The easiest way to put on your aqualung is to stand it upright on a flat surface at about hip height. Check the cylinder is switched fully on and that your pressure gauge indicates enough air inside. Then turn your back and bend at the knees, sitting against the edge of the support, and push both arms through the shoulder straps. In this way you do not have to support the full weight of the cylinder while you do up the waist strap.

Do not tighten the shoulder straps until you stand up and check that the demand valve is comfortably placed between your shoulder blades. Always check that the quick release mechanism of the waist strap functions properly.

Weight Belts

A weight belt is a necessary part of diving equipment. It counteracts the natural buoyancy of the body and diving suit.

The lead weights come in one-, two- or three-kilo sizes. Try to remember the weight that you have used, entering it in your log book. Remember that you will need about two kilos more weight in sea water.

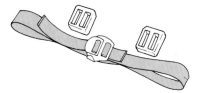

Above: The 'French' type weight belt has a 'D' shaped piece which can be removed to fit the weights. It is then re-threaded on to the belt and hooks through the widest part of the buckle, folding back flat. A slight push of the thumb is enough to release it.

Above: 'American' type weight belts and waist straps feature a metal clamp on one end. Make sure the belt can be released in an emergency.

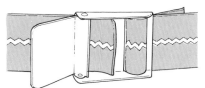

Above: With the 'American' system, one end is threaded through the catch, while the other is pushed under a clamp and tightened before closing.

Always guard against taking too much weight.

All weight belts have a quick-release buckle. The three main types are the *French, American* and *Loop* releases.

The advantage of the French type is that it releases instantly and weights are not liable to slip off if the belt is lifted by the 'wrong' end. The American kind is virtually the same as an airline seat belt, and involves pulling through any surplus belt in an emergency.

The wire loop kind can also work well although the loop may tend to become confused with other equipment.

Weight belts should be worn so that they cannot be snagged by other equipment.

Lifejackets

A good lifejacket is essential as it can both lift you back to the surface and support you once there. It also helps to maintain buoyancy on the bottom.

There are three main types: the Surface Lifejacket (SLJ), the Buoyancy Compensator (BC) and the Adjustable Buoyancy Lifejacket (ABLJ). Of these, however, only the ABLJ provides all the functions necessary to cope with diving emergencies.

Surface Lifejacket (SLJ)

The SLJ is similar to a yachting lifejacket and has a small cylinder of carbon dioxide which can be used in an emergency to inflate the lifejacket. It may also have a tube to allow inflation by mouth.

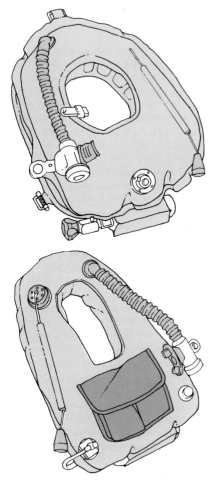

This type of lifejacket will support a diver adequately on the surface but it cannot lift him to the surface because there is only enough gas to fill the lifejacket at surface pressure.

Buoyancy Compensator (BC)

This type of lifejacket is operated by blowing compressed air from the aqualung cylinder into the lifejacket by means of a 'direct feed', which is a lead from the demand valve, operated by a push button.

The BC provides three functions:
1. It brings the diver up from depth in an emergency.
2. It can be used to adjust buoyancy at depth if the diver is too heavy.
3. It supports the diver on the surface.

Lifejackets are normally worn under all other equipment so that they can be used to provide buoyancy even if all other equipment is jettisoned. Some new American BCs, however, are attached to the aqualung and act as a comfortable jacket harness.

The disadvantage of the BC is that it depends on the main cylinder for air supply.

Adjustable Buoyancy Lifejacket (ABLJ)

The adjustable buoyancy lifejacket includes a small, completely separate cylinder of compressed air at the bottom of the jacket. This can be turned on in an emergency to provide independent 'lift off'. The cylinder is filled from the aqualung cylinder before each dive. So really this is the only lifejacket which is ideal for sport diving.

Above: Two adjustable buoyancy lifejackets (ABLJs). The controls for adjusting buoyancy are at the lower end of the corrugated tube. The emergency inflation cylinder is at the bottom of the jacket and the emergency 'dump' valve has a 'toggle' end to pull.

Wet Suits

The main function of a diving suit is to keep the diver warm, though they have their uses even in tropical waters where they may give protection against coral cuts and stings.

Wet suits come in a variety of thicknesses according to the amount of protection needed against cold. For British waters they should be at least 6 mm (¼ in) thick. Suits for pool training or warm tropical waters need only be 3 mm (⅛ in) thick.

Shorty Suits

'Shorty' suits are available for warm holiday diving but wet suits normally consist of trousers, jacket and bootees. The suits are made of closed-cell expanded neoprene, a spongy material which minimises heat loss.

The Trousers

The trousers, which are put on first, may finish at the waist or be extended into long johns which have an attached vest bringing added warmth.

The Bootees

The bootees are also neoprene and must have a hard rubber sole if you expect to walk over rocks or beaches. The bootees are tucked in under the trousers so that water tends not to enter when swimming.

Right: The diver's wet suit must cover him completely, especially in cold waters. This jacket has an off-centre reversed zip and attached hood. Bootees and gloves will complete the suit when diving in really cold water.

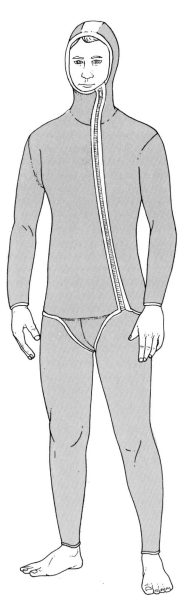

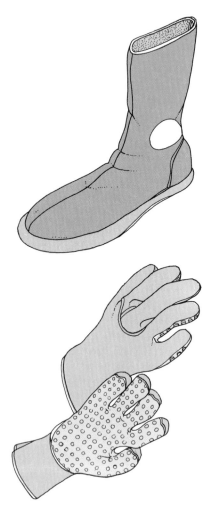

The Jacket

The jacket usually has a front zip for easy fitting. Cold water suits have an attached hood. The back is extended downwards in a flap which pulls between the legs and is fixed to the front of the suit by studs (this prevents the jacket rucking up during the dive).

Wet suits are ideal for tropical and sub-tropical diving and quite adequate for British summer conditions. Although they are sometimes used in winter, there is a warmer alternative in the dry suit.

Dry Suits

For British water temperatures, especially in winter, a dry suit will keep the diver much warmer than a wet suit. There can be complications with a dry suit, however, so it must be used carefully (see page 26).

Membrane and Neoprene Suits

There are two kinds of dry suit, the *membrane* suit made of lightweight rubberised material and the *neoprene* dry suit. Both these suits are made in one piece and have rolled seals at the wrists, neck and, if attached bootees are not supplied, at the ankles.

The 'Woolly Bear'

Although both suits should keep you dry, the membrane suit, particularly, needs an undersuit to keep you warm. This is known as a 'woolly bear'.

Membrane suits are cheaper and lighter, but the neoprene equivalent will provide better insulation in extreme conditions.

Above: Bootees and wet suit gloves are usually made of neoprene and protect the parts that get cold most quickly! Gloves will also protect the hands from sharp rocks and stings.

'WOOLLY BEAR'

Above: The 'woolly bear' undersuit keeps the dry-suited diver warm. It is made of polyester acrylic fibre. Some areas have extra padding for strength and warmth.

Above right: A 'membrane' dry suit is less robust than the neoprene equivalent but is much lighter in weight. The dry suit is kept waterproof by seals inside the cuffs and at the neck and ankles.

MEMBRANE DRY SUIT

Inlet and Outlet Tubes

When diving, the atmospheric air trapped in the suit becomes compressed and squeezes against your body. You become less buoyant, therefore inlet and outlet tubes must be fitted so that the air pressure inside can be adjusted. Air can then be let in through the air intake valve which is connected to the demand valve by a direct feed.

Once the diver turns towards the surface the air will begin to expand again and some should be vented from the exhaust valve to prevent 'ballooning up.'

Preventing Problems

Problems can occur if too much weight has been used and the diver has compensated by blowing a lot of air into the suit. If he then gets into a position in which his feet are higher than his head, the air may migrate into his boots and expand. If care is not taken the diver will then be on his way to the surface feet first!

Training drills in pool and sea can teach you how to overcome this predicament. It should not happen if the minimum air necessary to prevent squeezing is let into the suit and the diver pays attention to his position in the water.

Open Water Diving Equipment

When diving in open and deeper water some other pieces of equipment are necessary.

The first essential is a diving knife. This is not to attack or even provide a defence against sharks – but is needed in case you are trapped in fishing nets or weed. Modern fine

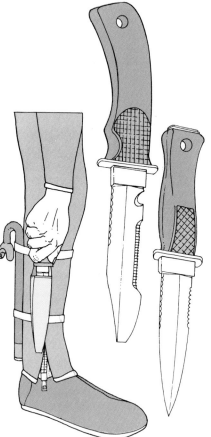

Above: Stainless steel diving knives may be worn on the calf or the upper arm. Knives should have sharp cutting edges so that the diver can slash himself free if he is entangled. Some more practical models include bottle opener and chisel or screwdriver tips. There should always be a catch that prevents the knife falling out when the diver is head down.

filament gill nets can be a death trap for an unwary diver, and a good serrated cutting edge is therefore vital. Knives may be strapped to the diver's calf. These straps then provide a useful place to push the snorkel tube which may be in the way if kept in the mask strap.

Depth Gauge
A depth gauge allows you to read off your exact depth below the surface at any time. Most depth gauges are oil-filled and temperature compensated. Those designed for the British market have indications every one or two metres to tie in with the BSAC/RNPL tables and have the five and 10 metre stops clearly marked.

Timing Devices
For safe diving you also need to know the time elapsed since you left the surface. This may be indicated by a *diving watch* or a *dive timer*.

The watch is pressure-proofed and should feature a movable 'bezel' round the outside which can be set when the diver leaves the surface, so that the minute hand shows clearly the number of minutes elapsed.

Alternatively a specially designed dive timer will start automatically when you go down and sound an alarm note when the scheduled dive time is reached.

Right: An oil-filled depth gauge with clear markings to 50 metres is essential. Those for dark waters are luminous.

A dive timer is easier to read and often cheaper than a diving watch.

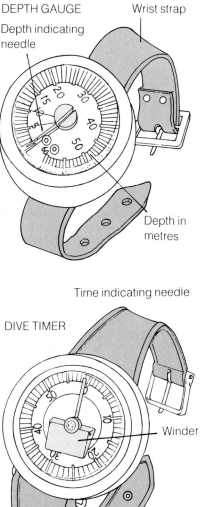

DEPTH GAUGE — Wrist strap
Depth indicating needle
Depth in metres

Time indicating needle
DIVE TIMER
Winder
Wrist strap

Useful Extras

Compasses can be extremely useful if you are diving from an anchored boat. A bearing can be taken before leaving so that divers can follow a planned route over the bottom.

Sometimes it is useful just to know the course which will take you out to sea (deeper) or towards the shore.

With practice a compass makes a diver more aware of his position and it is a highly desirable piece of equipment to have.

Torch

Torches are essential for night diving. During the day they can also light up the true colours in holes and caves where sunlight is filtered out.

Torches also allow the diver to examine wrecks and can be very varied in size from light, compact hand torches that give pencil beams to large lamps of great power.

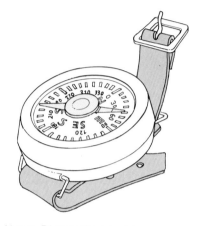

Above: Divers take a bearing on an object before leaving an anchored boat. They can then swim with the compass strapped on the arm which is bent in front of them, keeping the compass at a constant angle.

Below and right: Underwater torches are specially designed to resist pressure as well as be waterproof. They will not help in murky water as the beam will just illuminate the particles as in a fog. Colours disappear through the spectrum as depth increases, most of the reds being lost by 10 metres (33 feet). Torches enable the diver to see these colours again.

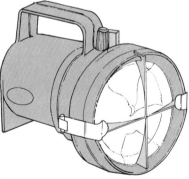

Surface Marker Buoy (SMB)

A surface marker buoy (SMB) is necessary when diving in tidal conditions or currents. It consists of an easily visible float with a short mast flying the diver's flag (see right). This is attached by a light line to a reel held by the dive leader. When the dive leader starts down, the reel is allowed to unwind. The line is kept taut or well away from other divers who might get entangled.

On arrival at the bottom the line is locked so that it cannot unwind any further and the dive can begin. The dive leader checks that everyone is OK and then swims or drifts off along the bottom followed by his companion or companions. The line, of course, drifts above and behind him pulling the buoy along the surface to mark the position of the divers. The cover boat, frequently an inflatable dinghy, will follow the buoy. Thus using a surface marker buoy allows divers to operate in quite strong currents without having to worry about being swept too far from the cover boat.

When the dive is finished, the dive leader reels in the line and the divers surface, knowing that the SMB has marked their position.

Right: The braced 'Flag A' can be seen above the wave tops as the mast holds it above the float. The weight on the bottom helps to keep the mast in an upright position. The floating line is attached to a plastic reel which is free to unwind as the divers descend, but can be checked with a catch when they reach the bottom, so that it stops paying out.

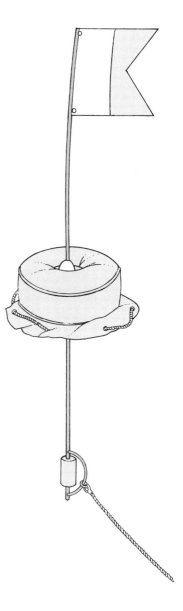

Diver's Slate

A diver's slate (such as the one produced by the BSAC) not only provides a surface to write notes and messages that cannot be communicated by underwater hand signals, but also includes a decompression table for planning and checking your dive. The slate should fit comfortably into the pocket of an ABLJ.

PRACTICAL TRAINING
Using an Aqualung

Your first lesson in a pool or sheltered water should be with a qualified instructor.

You begin by kneeling in the shallows with your head just below water level, breathing from the aqualung and convincing yourself that it really works!

Then you start swimming, using just your fins to move you along, leaving your arms trailing or using them as a buffer to keep you off the bottom.

Exercises

Your first exercise will show you how to adjust your buoyancy by breathing. You will discover that when you breathe out fully, you lose buoyancy and tend to sink and when you hold your breath in you tend to become lighter.

The second exercise is to remove your mouthpiece underwater. Kneel on the bottom, take a breath in, hold it, and take out your mouthpiece. It may bubble with air depending on the position it is in. After a few seconds put it back into your mouth and breathe out into it again.

Now you are ready to try mask clearing. Sooner or later your mask will leak and water will collect in the bottom. You may even have it knocked off by another diver's fins! You must be able to clear it without having to swim up to the surface.

To practise this, kneel on the bottom and let in a little water by lifting the mask slightly at the bottom. Then press your fingers against the top of the face plate to set it against your forehead, and start breathing out from your nose into the mask. You can take several breaths: in through the mouth and out through the nose (eventually you will do this in one breath only). The air that you blow from your nose will fill the mask and, as it cannot escape at the top where you are pressing, it will be forced out at the bottom taking the water with it. As you start to blow, tilt your head back to make sure that the last of the water collected against your upper lip is blown out.

Above: The diver presses the top of his mask to his forehead as he blows out through his nose to expel water.

Part 2 Signals

Hand Signals

Before you go down on your first dive you must know the recognised international hand signals used by all divers. Although it is possible to take out the mouthpiece and speak briefly into the water, the result is usually unintelligible so signals are used to pass the most important messages from diver to diver.

The first three signals are concerned with the diver's well-being:
1. *Are you OK?* This is the most used signal and is done with the thumb and forefinger making a circle and the other fingers held together vertically upwards behind. Most signals can be done with either hand. The reply, *Yes I am OK*, is the same signal returned by the other diver.

This signal is also used to mean *OK, I understand*, in response to some other signal.
2. *Something is wrong* or *Something is going wrong* The hand is held steady and rocked to and fro on its axis. This should result in another diving swimming up to see if they can give help. The first diver may then point to the problem area.
3. *Help!* This is a serious signal when assistance is required urgently. It is shown by waving the hand with fingers clenched.

Right: As it is impossible to speak intelligibly underwater, it is vital to know the basic signals which are recognised by all divers. Single arm signals can be done with either arm. Always remember to respond promptly to signals from the leader.

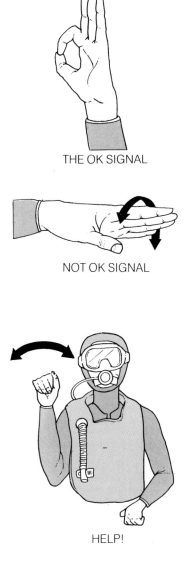

THE OK SIGNAL

NOT OK SIGNAL

HELP!

Three signals connected with the diver's breathing and air supply:
1. *Short of air* The clenched fist raised and held steady level with the face with the fingers towards the other diver indicates that you are beginning to get short of air.

The signal will normally be aimed at the dive leader who should collect any other divers together and take everyone slowly back to the surface.

2. *No air at all* The signal is a flattened hand in a horizontal plane making 'chopping' movements against the throat. It indicates the diver has no air at all! This is a rare occurrence, luckily, but could happen if you have not watched the pressure gauge.

There is no time to reply to the signal other than by swimming up to the distressed diver and passing him your mouthpiece so that he can share your air (see page 49).

3. *Out of breath* This signal is given by moving both hands in and out from the lungs at the same time to indicate rapid breathing. This means that you are out of breath or panting.

The response to the out of breath signal from the dive leader should be the *Stop* signal (like a traffic policeman's Halt signal) – hand raised palm towards you.

Other divers in the group should also be stopped so that you can rest before continuing more slowly.

Right: A regular air supply is vital to a diver. Training will bring the confidence to enable you to signal calmly when in any difficulties.

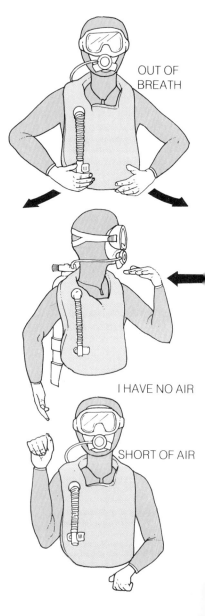

OUT OF BREATH

I HAVE NO AIR

SHORT OF AIR

Direction Signals

There are three direction signals:

1. *Go up! Let's go up* or *I am going up* is shown by the thumbs up sign.

2. *Going down* etc the thumbs down signal.

3. *Direction to swim* is shown by pointing an index finger. This last signal pointed at the diver also means *You*, or pointed at oneself *Me*.

Surfacing

When a diver has made the signal that he is getting short of air, or the dive leader wants to finish the dive for another reason such as cold or decompression time, he will beckon the divers to come together, point at each in turn, then at himself and give the *Go up* signal.

Divers should 'fin' up slowly, not travelling faster than their small exhaust bubbles, all the time facing each other and checking occasionally with signals that all is OK.

If they have been venting air into their lifejackets or dry suits to make them lighter on the bottom, they should remember to release this air slowly on the way up. The dive leader should keep an eye on his depth gauge and slow down as they approach the surface.

In good visibility, the divers should position themselves so that they can scan the surface from underneath to check for approaching boats or other hazards.

Right: Dive leaders always check on the surface that everyone is OK before making the 'Go down' signal. They also decide when to come up.

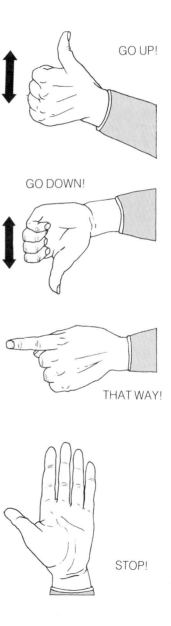

GO UP!

GO DOWN!

THAT WAY!

STOP!

In poor visibility, they should surface with hands above their heads in case they strike an obstacle.

Once on the surface, they swing round to look out for boats and to make contact with the cover boat.

Signal Flags

The diver's marker buoy should be surmounted by the blue and white 'A' flag from the International Code of Signals. The alternative meaning of the flag is *I have a diver down, keep clear and at slow speed.*

The dive boat should also show this signal whenever divers are down. One of the biggest hazards to surfacing is an approaching boat which has not seen you in the water.

At American dive sites an alternative flag (red with one diagonal white stripe) may be used although strictly speaking this is now obsolete.

Signalling the Cover Boat

The two surface signals from divers to their boat are made using the whole arm so that the signal can be

Above: A diver who is trapped may often be easily freed by his companion. The emergency banging on the cylinder will bring help from divers some distance away. If you don't have a knife, use a stone .

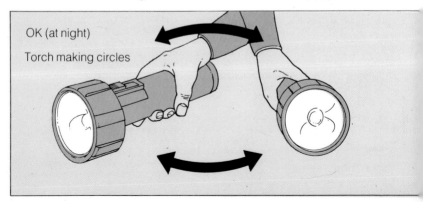

OK (at night)

Torch making circles

seen at a distance. If divers are operating in tidal waters using a buoy, and being tracked by their boat, an arm raised straight up in the air with the fingers making the OK signal means *We are OK and are over here, please pick us up as soon as possible*. It is acknowledged by the same signal from the boat.

If the boat is picking up other divers at the same time you may have to wait. If so, stay together and let air into your lifejackets to make it easier to rest.

Immediate Pick Up
If divers arrive back on the surface and need immediate assistance, the diver leader will wave his arm indicating *Help! We need you now*.

In case of difficulty, but not emergency, the static OK signal can be followed by a slowly waving arm.

Other forms of signalling
Although the first rule of diving is Never Dive Alone, exceptions may be made for very experienced divers who are connected by line to

a surface tender, in the same way as a helmet diver would be. An agreed code of signals (tugs on the line) is set out in the *BSAC Manual*.

Signalling in the Dark
At night you can see with the aid of a torch, and, if it is a dark night, you see little that is not actually lit by the beam. Signals can be made in the beam although this takes two hands. It may be better to improvise special night signals such as:
1. Torch swung in circles means *Are you OK?* and *OK*.
2. Torch swung slowly up and down on surface means *We are OK and ready to be picked up*.
3. At the surface, torch swung from side to side *Help, pick us up now!*
Always try to avoid shining your torch directly into someone's eyes!

Below: Night dives can be a fascinating experience especially in warm, clear waters. Different animals appear and some fish actually sleep on the bottom. You should not dive until you are used to your equipment.

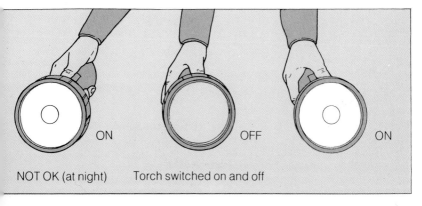

NOT OK (at night)   Torch switched on and off

Part 3 Hazards – how to overcome them

Overcoming Hazards Underwater

We live in an air pressure of one atmosphere (1 bar) which represents the weight of air in the atmosphere surrounding the earth. To lessen this pressure it is necessary to rise many thousands of metres above the earth until there is no atmosphere at all.

However, we have only to go down underwater to a depth of 10 metres (33 feet) to *double* the pressure we are in. For every 10 metres travelled downwards in the sea, another atmosphere of pressure is added:

10 m (33 ft) = 2ats absolute pressure (surface + 1)

20 m (66 ft) = 3ats absolute pressure (S + 2)

30 m (99 ft) = 4ats absolute pressure (S + 3)

Demonstrating Underwater Pressure

This increased pressure can be demonstrated quite dramatically by taking an empty but sealed drinks can down to 10 metres (33 feet). It will be completely crushed by the water pressure acting on the atmospheric pressure inside the can. A balloon will be similarly affected, although, of course, it would be able to regain its original shape when returned to the surface.

Body Composition

The body is mainly composed of water and is therefore virtually incompressible underwater. But there are air spaces within the body which are sometimes of fixed volume (like a can) and sometimes capable of change in shape (like a balloon).

The sinuses, for instance, are holes in the bone structure of our heads and therefore cannot alter shape whilst the lungs can and do change shape all the time and can adjust to increasing pressure.

Descending

The changing pressure and volume of air affect the air spaces inside the diver more strongly near the surface than in deeper water (see the explanation of Boyle's Law opposite). This is why a diver's ears hurt quite soon if they swim down underwater without adjusting the pressure inside. The section on page 41 shows you how to clear your ears easily.

Surfacing

Coming up towards the surface, exactly the same happens but in reverse. You can see, therefore, that although the *pressure* change from 70 metres (230 feet) to 60 metres (197 feet) is the same as that from 10 metres (33 feet) to the surface (1at), the *volume* change of the air deep down will be much less than in the last layers before the surface.

You must never hold your breath when you come up using an aqualung or the large increase in air volume in your lungs, which occurs once near the surface, may cause serious problems (pages 44–47)

Hazards of Surface Depths

Boyle's Law, therefore, is all important in diving, demonstrating that in some ways the surface depths can be more hazardous to divers, than the deeper ones.

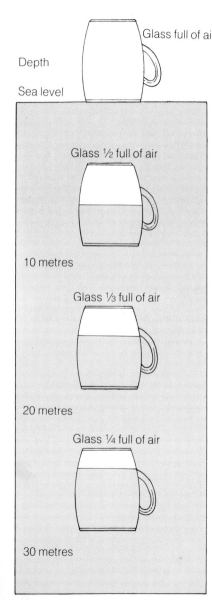

Depth

Sea level

Glass full of air

Pressure
1 atmosphere

Glass ½ full of air

10 metres

Pressure 2 ats
(doubled)

Glass ⅓ full of air

20 metres

Pressure 3 ats
(tripled)

Glass ¼ full of air

30 metres

Pressure 4 ats
(quadrupled)

Boyle's Law

If you up-end an empty glass and lower it gently into water, you will trap a whole glass full of air inside at atmospheric pressure. If you then

push it gently downwards, so as not to spill any air, to a depth of 10 metres (33 feet) you will have doubled the pressure (1at to 2ats), and if you look into the glass you will see that you have halved the volume of air inside i.e. the water has risen to fill half the glass.

Moving on down to 20 metres (66 feet) the pressure will increase to three times (1at to 3ats). The water will have risen to fill two-thirds of the glass and the air will be reduced to a third of its original volume.

At 30 metres (99 feet) the volume of air will be reduced from a third to a quarter. The greater the depth, the less the change in air volume will be.

Adjusting Air Spaces in the Body

There are a number of air spaces in the body which can be affected by the increasing and decreasing pressures as we move through the underwater layers.

The lungs and the passages connecting them to the aqualung are, of course, kept artificially at the same pressure as the surrounding water by means of the demand valve.

There are, however, small pockets of gas in the stomach and intestines. These should not cause a problem providing that you are careful not to swallow air which will then pass into the stomach. Divers, of course, must breathe through their mouths when underwater, but the air should go straight to the lungs. If you manage to swallow while breathing underwater, the air will go into the stomach. Then, as you rise to the surface, the air will expand as the water pressure lessens and you may be 'blown up' with wind like a baby! A good belch will usually relieve this condition.

It is also possible to get toothache underwater. This is caused by air pressure in a tiny cavity, often where a filling has moved a bit. If air is trapped and cannot equalize to the surrounding atmosphere it may cause pain. The only cure for this problem is a visit to the dentist on your return to the surface.

Mask Squeeze

If you alter depth suddenly by swimming downwards or, if you accidentally breathe in through your nose instead of your mouth, the air pressure in your mask will drop and it will be sucked in against your face. Although this may not be too painful, it is important to counteract the 'squeeze' by blowing some air from the nose into the mask.

If this is not done, and the diver continues with the mask sucked against his face, the drop in pressure can damage the small blood vessels under the skin and in the eyes, resulting in red marks on the whites of the eyes and also black eyes. Usually this isn't serious although it looks unattractive but it can develop into a serious condition.

Always check that your mask is not too tight and that there is enough air inside.

Air Spaces in the Body

Right: The body's air spaces present few problems on the surface but once water pressure increases they may cause difficulties for the diver.

The aqualung is directly connected to the lungs via the mouth and trachea (or windpipe) and these air spaces are thus kept at the same pressure as the surrounding water.

The other air spaces in the head are connected to one another – the nasal cavity, the eustachian tubes, the sinuses and the ears – and these do cause problems when underwater.

Ear 'clearing' is a skill that all divers need to develop (see page 41) and, similarly, they may need to clear the sinuses (see page 44).

Any nasal congestion will increase difficulties with clearing and so diving with a bad cold is inadvisable.

Divers occasionally swallow air but this can be easily 'burped' up from the stomach.

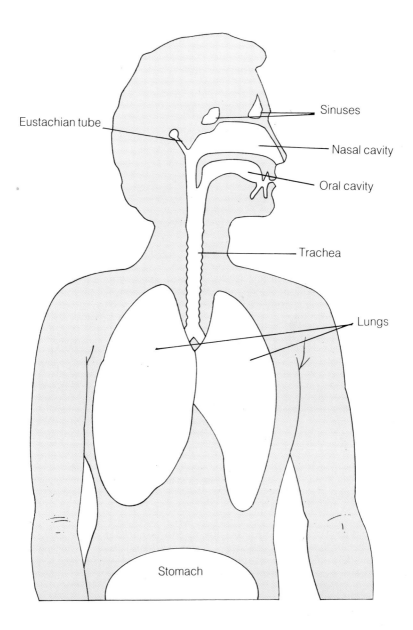

Sinuses

Eustachian tube

Nasal cavity

Oral cavity

Trachea

Lungs

Stomach

The Ear

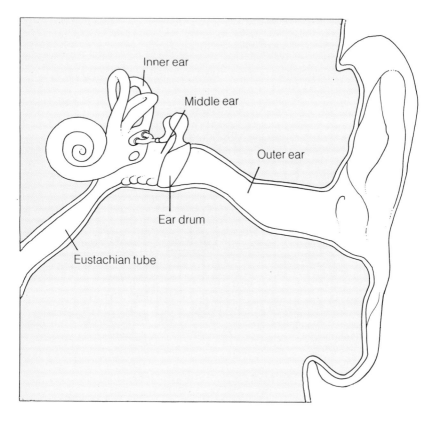

Inner ear

Middle ear

Outer ear

Ear drum

Eustachian tube

Above: There are three main parts to the ear:

The outer ear which is the part that you can see together with the passage leading in to the ear drum. The ear drum separates the outer ear from the middle and inner sections.

The middle ear is an air chamber on the other side of the drum which is connected by a small tube – the eustachian tube – to the back of the nose and throat.

The inner ear is found inside the middle ear and is a complicated and delicate organ which controls the sense of balance.

Problems occur when you go underwater. The water runs into the outer ear passage, and the increasing pressure begins to bend the ear drum inwards. The pain warns you that you need to 'clear'.

Clearing the Ears when Diving

To 'clear' ears when underwater, the diver must swim up slightly to lessen the pain, seal off the nose by holding it firmly through the mask, and blow *gently* through it. The air pressure should open up the eustachian tube and blow some air into the middle ear on the other side of the drum to equalise the pressure, thus stopping the pain.

Some divers are lucky enough to be able to do this by swallowing and waggling their jaws, but most find it easier using this 'seal and blow' method.

One of the most common fears that beginners have is that, because their ears hurt when they go underwater, they will be unable to dive. This is not so, but ears *are* very delicate and, besides enabling you to hear, they also control your balance and sense of position. Never dive if you have an ear infection and make sure you dry your ears thoroughly afterwards.

If you ever do have a burst ear drum it should heal up well, but you need to have a medical examination before diving again.

Come up to Shallow Water

If your ears do not 'clear', come up into shallower water and try again until they do.

Never force them because others are waiting for you on the bottom or for any other reason.

Ear Plugs

Never wear ear plugs underwater. The increasing pressure would force them into your ears (see right).

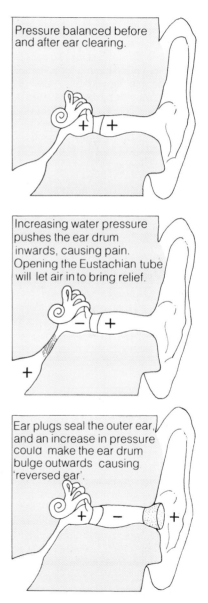

Pressure balanced before and after ear clearing.

Increasing water pressure pushes the ear drum inwards, causing pain. Opening the Eustachian tube will let air in to bring relief.

Ear plugs seal the outer ear, and an increase in pressure could make the ear drum bulge outwards causing 'reversed ear'.

Methods of Descent

After you have dived down below the surface layers, you will have less trouble with your ears. This is because you have such a large volume of air behind the ear drum that little adjustment will be needed later (remember Boyle's Law). When you come up after the dive, the extra air should escape again with no problem.

Prevention

About 20% of divers have noticeably more problem in clearing their ears than the others. If you are among them, or, if you want to prevent the pain happening at all, there are some ways to make diving 'easier on the ears'.

1. Clearing every Metre

Don't wait for them to hurt. As soon as your head goes under, start holding your nose and clearing gently. Do this every metre or so until you arrive at the bottom. With luck this will prevent the difference in pressure building up.

2. Diving Feet First

Although it is exhilarating to glide down, head first, especially in warm, clear waters, if you have ear troubles it may be better to start head up on the surface. Exhale to help yourself go down and sink away *feet first*, clearing your ears as you go. In this way the ears are not put into the deeper layers first and clearing should be easier. Remember to take things very slowly and move up to shallower water at any sign of trouble.

Above: The diver who has difficulty with his ears can go down feet first and 'clear' continually from the surface.

Right: The author (left) discovered one of the oldest wrecks in the world off Giglio in Italy. Here he and archaeologist Mensun Bound stop their descent on the shot line to clear ears and check equipment.

3. Diving from a Boat or Buoy Line

If you are diving from an anchored boat or down a buoy line or pole, hold on to it with one hand. This will allow you to maintain an exact depth. As your ears react, you can move up or down, hand over hand, changing the depth gradually and carefully.

Sinuses

The sinuses are connected to the ear chambers and normally 'clear' when you clear your ears. If they do not, you will soon realise, because they cause a sharp pain, usually in the frontal sinuses, above the eyebrow line. Treat this pain as you would an ear pain, by swimming up slightly and trying to clear. You may have to go nearly to the surface before there is a squeak and the air gets into the sinuses.

Medical Checks

Before diving in open water, it is essential that you have a medical and chest X-ray. The *BSAC Medical Form* gives guidance to GPs; a medical is valid for five years up to the age of 30, three years to 50, and annually thereafter.

Although burst ear drums may seal over again quite strongly, those who have a chronic perforated drum should not dive without getting it repaired.

The lungs and heart should be normal and divers should not suffer from diabetes or epilepsy. In cases of doubt, a diving medical referee should be consulted. A list of referees is available from the BSAC headquarters (see page 79).

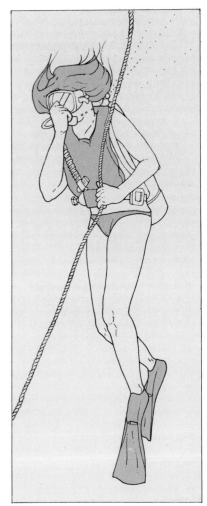

Using an Anchor Line

A diver who has problems with ear clearing can make use of an anchor line. This will act as a guide to lowering yourself so that you vary the depth slightly after each 'clear'.

The Lungs

Breathing and Circulation

The air we breathe is made up of 79% nitrogen, 21% oxygen and lesser amounts of carbon dioxide (CO_2) and other gases. The oxygen in the air is absorbed through the alveoli (thin bubble-like membranes at the lung surface) and is picked up by the red corpuscles in the blood and carried round the body.

Oxygen is needed to activate the muscles for daily life. During this time, some of the oxygen is changed into CO_2, and when it returns to the lungs, it filters back through the alveoli and is breathed out. Exhaled air therefore has a higher percentage of CO_2 in it.

Air Cylinders

The amount of air you can carry depends not only on the aqualung's size but on the pressure of air pumped into it. An average cylinder for open water use has a capacity of 10 litres. If this is filled to a pressure of 200 atmospheres, there will be 2,000 litres of air in it when full (10×200). This is equivalent to 75 cubic feet (cylinders are still known as '75s').

Cylinders are made of steel or aluminium alloy. Steel is usually lighter and tougher, but may rust internally. The aluminium equivalent has a thicker wall and so may be heavier. Corrosion of aluminium cylinders is less likely but rapid when it occurs.

Cylinders are manufactured and tested to government regulations. Markings are stamped on the shoulder or neck. These show the manufacturers mark and number, the government specification, date of manufacture, capacity, working pressure and marks and dates of subsequent tests. The BSAC recommends that cylinders are inspected every year. If you buy a secondhand cylinder, get one with date stamps and a test certificate from a well-established testing station.

Air Consumption

The amount of air you actually use underwater varies enormously from person to person according to sex, size and experience of diving. Consumption will also increase if work is being done, if the diver is swimming against a current or if the dive is in cold water.

An average breathing rate of a man swimming on the surface might be 25 litres per minute. At a depth of 10 m (33 ft) – double the pressure – the demand valve will give him twice as much air. At 20 metres (66 ft) three times as much and so on. This theoretical rate of air consumption is, however, of little value because of the variations in diver and conditions. It is vital to check your pressure gauge regularly during a dive.

Burst Lung

One of the most important things to remember is that when you breathe compressed air underwater at the same pressure as the surrounding water you must not hold your breath when you swim back to the surface.

This does not normally occur, of course, but if a diver panics when short of air, for instance, the instinct

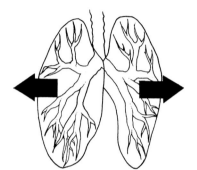

Above: Holding the breath while ascending with an aqualung will result in the alveoli stretching and spillage of air into blood or tissues.

may be to hold his breath.

If a diver is short of air and isn't near enough another diver to operate the normal sharing system, he should start for the surface letting air out in a gentle stream, like whistling.

If the breath is held, the compressed air in the lungs expands as the water pressure lessens and the lungs are 'blown up'. Eventually some air will spill out of the overstretched lungs, this is called burst lung and sometimes causes serious damage.

A diver can only suffer from burst lung when breathing from compressed air, so snorkellers are not affected. Remember, though, never to let a snorkeller take a breath from your aqualung mouthpiece when he is underwater.

Results of Burst Lung

There are three kinds of burst lung, each depends on where the air is forced to go after it leaves the lung.

Air Embolism

The most serious result of burst lung is called *air embolism* and this occurs when the escaping air enters directly into the blood stream causing air bubbles to form. The bubbles are carried round the body in the blood and small bubbles may combine together to make large ones and, if a large bubble comes into contact with the heart, you can lose interest in events fairly permanently! The bubbles may lodge in other parts of the body too, causing serious damage by blocking off the blood supply.

Pneumothorax and Emphysema

If the air spills into the area between the lungs and the chest wall, the condition, which is slightly less serious, is called *pneumothorax*.

When the expanding air bursts into the tissues between and above the lungs, the result is known as *emphysema*.

Symptoms

The symptoms of burst lung are wide ranging. A distressed diver with air embolism may have breathing problems and be affected by giddiness, numbness, paralysis, double vision and even heart failure.

Symptoms of pneumothorax are shortness of breath, coughing blood, pain when breathing, swollen chest and blue-grey skin colour (*cyanosis*).

Those with emphysema may suffer from shortness of breath accompanied by difficulty in swallowing, and swelling at the base of the neck.

The exact symptoms, however, are not important. They usually appear quite soon (two or three minutes in the case of air embolism) after surfacing.

The important thing to remember is: any symptoms after an unusual or rushed ascent – suspect burst lung.

Immediate Treatment

·The only recommended treatment is to take the casualty to the nearest recompression chamber immediately.

These are found at Navy bases that are involved with diving, such as *HMS Vernon* at Portsmouth and *HMS Drake* at Plymouth.

HMS Vernon keeps a list of all operational chambers in Britain and in emergency a priority call should be made to the Duty Officer on 0705-818888.

Chambers are also found in the North Sea diving industry centres (such as Aberdeen) and at the larger sport diving centres such as Stoney Cove in the Midlands.

They are expensive installations which you cannot expect to find on small islands where you have booked your diving holiday.

Recompression Chambers

A recompression chamber is basically a large high pressure cylinder which contains a pressure proof door with pipes through which compressed air can be pumped. The chamber has a heavy glass window, an intercom to the outside and a bed. Often it has two doors, one inside the other, which enclose a 'lock' so that a doctor, for instance, can be 'blown down' in the lock to equal pressure so that he can attend the casualty.

Below: This diagram of a recompression chamber shows the intercom, window and pressure gauge. The small 'lock' has just been pressurized so that the doctor can open the inner door.

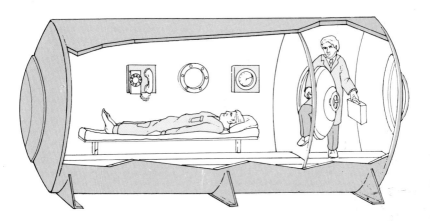

Once the distressed diver is in the chamber air is rapidly pumped in. As the air pressure increases towards the pressure at which the diver began his breath-holding ascent, the air bubbles should grow smaller until they disappear. The air pressure is then reduced very slowly, so that the bubbles do not reform. The diver may be in the chamber for many hours, but food and drink can be passed in through a small 'lock' in the side.

Casualties being Flown
If casualties have to be flown to a chamber, it is important that special permission is sought to fly low to prevent bubbles in the blood becoming larger because of the drop in air pressure. The diver should be laid on his left side with the head lower than the feet to encourage the bubbles away from the heart and head.

How to surface without Air
If you find yourself without air in an emergency there are four ways of reaching the surface safely:

1. Octopus Rig
This is the easiest and least taxing method of surfacing and uses a piece of equipment known as an *octopus rig*.
   This is an extra second stage or mouthpiece attached to the demand valve with a slightly longer tube. The spare mouthpiece is either fixed to the front of the diver's suit with an easy quick release, or stowed in the ABLJ pocket. Then, if a diver runs out of air, he can swim to

Above: The 'octopus rig' in action. This is the easiest way of coming up without air. The diver whose 'octopus' is being used, holds the distressed diver close and they both ascend slowly to the surface.

Above: Sharing or 'buddy breathing'. The diver on the left is sharing her air with a companion who has run out of air. She keeps him close to her and holds on to her mouthpiece to direct the breathing rhythm.

the person with the octopus rig, pick up the spare mouthpiece and immediately start breathing. They can then both return slowly to the surface before the air cylinder (which they are both using) is emptied.

Although many instructors use octopus rigs, the cost and inconvenience of the extra equipment unfortunately deters divers from carrying them in order to assist their fellows.

2. Assisted Ascent (Sharing)

This technique (called 'buddy breathing' in the USA), involves two divers sharing a single mouthpiece from which they take it in turns to have two breaths each. The distressed diver makes the signal *I have no air at all* (see page 32). Then the assisting diver swims up, takes a quick breath and passes the mouthpiece across. The distressed diver takes two or three breaths before releasing it.

They settle down to a rhythm of two breaths each and then, when this has been established, start swimming slowly up to the surface, exhaling slightly when not breathing from the mouthpiece.

Both this and the octopus method are excellent ways to return to the surface, but sharing needs either an experienced partner or plenty of practice to be used successfully in a real emergency.

3. Free or Swimming Ascent

If the air-starved diver is far from other divers or, if he is accompanied by an inexperienced diver, it may be necessary to reach the surface without an air supply at all.

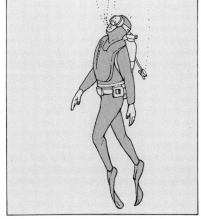

Above: A free ascent needs to be carefully controlled with the diver breathing out as though whistling. Alternatively he may keep the mouthpiece in place while he exhales.

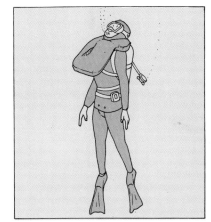

Above: Buoyant ascent using a compressed air lifejacket brings the diver up to the surface as fast as possible. He must breathe out steadily all the way to prevent burst lung.

In a free ascent, the diver swims steadily upwards, breathing out gently as he rises to prevent burst lung. This method can best be used when the diver can see the surface.

Free ascent needs great control and co-ordination which is very hard to achieve and so this technique cannot be recommended.

4. Buoyant Ascent

The fourth method is to use the ABLJ. The small compressed air cylinder is turned on until the jacket fills and the diver starts to 'lift off'. It should then be closed.

As the diver rises the air in the lifejacket will expand and his speed will increase to approximately six feet per second! It is therefore *vital* that he breathes out steadily all the way up.

The lifejacket, incidentally, will not explode as a result of the rapidly expanding air inside as the 'dump' valve will release it automatically.

Although an ascent at this speed can bring problems, including a great likelihood of burst lung and decompression sickness, it does return the diver to the surface quickly and, even if he is unconscious, the ABLJ will hold his head clear of the water when he arrives. It is the diver's ultimate safety device if all else fails.

Remember to always wear an ABLJ and always breathe out when you come up.

Right: An ancient amphora (storage jar) is brought up by two divers. Life jackets can provide extra buoyancy for lifting objects from the sea bed.

Decompression Sickness 'The Bends'

Air is composed mainly of the gases nitrogen, oxygen and carbon dioxide. The body only needs to extract oxygen from the air but 79% of the atmosphere is nitrogen.

On a deep dive so much nitrogen is taken into the lungs that it begins to dissolve in the blood and fatty tissues of the body. If the diver remains at depth for any length of time, and then returns directly to the surface, the blood may not be able to hold the nitrogen in solution and it will turn back to gas and form bubbles in the blood stream. It's exactly the same effect as when bottled drinks fizz as they are opened and the dissolved gas forms bubbles.

As already explained, bubbles in the blood (whether air or nitrogen) are potentially dangerous. Urgent recompression is essential to disperse them and the diver must be rushed to the nearest recompression chamber.

To prevent the bends, tables have been developed (see page 55) to give precise directions on how to surface without danger.

Symptoms

The symptoms of decompression sickness do not always show themselves as quickly as those of burst lung, but 50% of cases usually show themselves within half an hour of surfacing, 85% within one hour and 95% within three hours. The rest can be delayed for up to 24 hours.

Therefore it is important to know the symptoms as they may not appear immediately.

The most common symptom is pain in the joints. Pains are most likely to occur in joints that have been used while diving (eg knees). Pains are commonly felt in the shoulders. The feeling may vary from a dull ache to intense pain. Aches are sometimes preceded by itching and rashes or swellings on the hands. Helmet divers during the last century called these hand symptoms *ants* or *sheep*.

If a diver develops these rashes, which are minor symptoms, he should be carefully watched for the pain symptoms. If these do occur, then he needs to be taken to a recompression chamber.

If divers ignore the rules and the tables altogether they run the risk of the most serious symptoms, known to the helmet divers as *the staggers* and *the shakes*.

Difficulty in standing and controlling body movements is often followed by paralysis from the waist downwards or other very serious symptoms.

Helicopters or light aircraft should be summoned whenever possible and should fly the victim to the nearest chamber immediately. The diver should always be laid on his left side with his head lower than his feet and pure oxygen should be given if it is available.

Divers at Risk

The divers most at risk are those diving for gain. Sooner or later professional crawfish, coral, sponge or wreck divers find themselves being tempted to stay too long underwater to collect something extra.

DECOMPRESSED GASES

Right: Carbon dioxide gas is forced into 'fizzy drinks' under pressure. While the top is sealed the drink appears clear and bubble-free as the gas is completely dissolved.

Right: When the bottle is opened slowly, the pressure is released and the liquid can no longer contain the gas in solution. It begins to bubble.

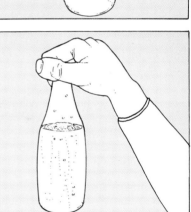

Right: If the pressure is released suddenly, the liquid will not only bubble but will froth. The aqualung diver's blood reacts in the same dramatic way if pressure changes are too sudden during ascent.

Prevention Tables

Preventing the Bends

A French scientist, Paul Bert, diagnosed the cause of decompression sickness, but the first practical work on prevention was done by Professor J S Haldane in Britain.

Haldane believed that the diver could return to half the pressure (or depth) of his dive as quickly as he liked, but then had to slow down drastically when he came close to the surface.

His *Decompression Tables* were the first devised and others were developed from them.

Descent and Ascent Rates

Descent and ascent rates are part of planned decompression. You should not go down faster than 30 metres a minute or come up faster than 15 metres a minute.

The ascent rate is particularly important especially if you are not in sight of a guideline, a cliff for example, but in open water.

In this case, turn around until you can see some of your exhaust bubbles. The biggest ones will tend to balloon up fast, but if you pick one of the smallest bubbles and come up with it, your rate of ascent will be roughly 15 metres per minute.

How to Use the BSAC/RNPL Table

The first two lefthand columns of the table give the time allowed at a particular depth without stops according to the maximum depth that is reached during the dive. For example, you could stay 46 minutes at 20 metres (66 feet), but only seven minutes at 50 metres (164 feet) without stops.

If the dive is in water shallower than 10 metres (33 feet), no times are given and the diver can remain indefinitely.

All the times on the table are *bottom times*. This time, however, is not just the time that can be spent on the bottom but *also includes* the time taken to reach the bottom.

Bottom time therefore, is the time from leaving the surface (when you first set timer or watch) until you leave the bottom to come up.

If you are diving to a depth not marked on the table, say 35 metres (115 feet) you round it up to the next depth shown ie 36 metres (118 feet). The bottom time for 35 metres is therefore 14 minutes.

It is better not to stay longer than this 'no stop' time unless there is a very good reason. Decompression stops can bring complications – you could be cold, exhausted or short of air at the end of the dive.

Advance Planning

If it is essential that you do a dive involving stops, then *plan it well beforehand.*

Put a shotline (a line with a weight or anchor at the bottom and a buoy at the top, to keep it vertical) on the exact place that you want to dive.

Then tie a spare aqualung on to the line at each of the depths of your stops so that if you get short of air, you can change mouthpieces and breath from this reserve cylinder.

Right: The BSAC/RNPL (Royal Navy Physiological Laboratory) air diving decompression table was the first to be produced for amateur divers.

DIVE DETAILS

Time _____ Depth _____ Duration _____

Time _____ Depth _____ Duration _____

RNPL/BSAC Air Diving Decompression Table

Descent Rate: 30 metres/minute maximum
Ascent Rate: 15 metres/minute

Maximum Depth (metres)	No Stop Time (minutes)	Bottom Time in Minutes					
		5	10	15	20	25	30
10	232	431	—	—	—	—	—
12	137	140	159	179	201	229	270
14	96	98	106	116	125	134	144
16	72	73	81	88	94	99	105
18	57	59	66	71	76	80	84
20	46	49	55	60	63	67	70

Stops at 5 metres (minutes)

Maximum Depth (metres)	No Stop Time (minutes)	5	10	15	20	25	30
22	38	42	47	51	55	58	
24	32	37	41	45	48	51	
26	27	32	37	40	43	45	
28	23	29	33	36	39	41	
30	20	25	30	33	35	37	
32	18	23	27	30	32	34	
34	16	21	25	28	30		
36	14	20	23	26			
38	12	18	21	24			
40	11	17	20	22	24	25	
42	10	16	19	21	22		
44	9	15	18	20	21		
46	8	14	17	18	20		
48	8	13	16	17			
50	7	12	15	17			

Stops at 10 metres / 5 metres (minutes): 5 | 5 | 5 | 5 | 5 | 5

Not more than 8 hours spent under pressure (submerged) during 24 hours

FOR TWO DIVES ONLY

When Second Dive is less than 9 metres no stop is required

A = Bottom Time in minutes of 1st Dive
B = Bottom Time in minutes of 2nd Dive

Both Dives less than 40 metres

Surface Interval	Bottom Time
Up to 2 hours	A + B
2 to 4 hours	A/2 + B
4 to 6 hours	A/4 + B
More than 6 hours	B

Either Dive more than 40 metres

Surface Interval	Bottom Time
Up to 2 hours	A + B
2 to 4 hours	A/2 + B
4 to 8 hours	A/4 + B
8 to 16 hours	A/8 + B
More than 16 hours	B

ALWAYS DECOMPRESS FOR THE GREATEST DEPTH REACHED DURING EITHER DIVE.

How to Work Out Stops

If you decide to dive to a depth of 20 metres (66 feet) for 60 minutes, find 20 metres in the left hand column and then follow the line across until you find 60 minutes. Then follow the column down until you find a white figure or figures (in this case 15). As you can see at the start of the black squares, this means that you must do a 15 minute stop just under the surface at a depth of five metres (16½ feet).

If, for example, you are diving on a wreck at 40 metres (131 feet) and have decided that 20 minutes is needed to photograph it, you find these figures in the table and, running down the column, see a white 5 and, below it, a white 10.

Thus, after doing this dive, you come up – at 15 metres (49 feet) a minute or the speed of the small bubbles – to a depth of 10 metres (33 feet) and wait there on the line until the timer has reached five minutes. You then reset it to zero and swim up to five metres (16½ feet) where you wait until it has reached 10 minutes.

Note that you start timing the stops from the moment that you leave the bottom or the previous stop.

Avoid Deep Dives

If you do long dives that involve decompression stops you will be more at risk from decompression sickness. No table is infallible, and resistance varies from day to day and from person to person.

Try to avoid deep dives and especially those involving decompression stops.

Calculating Other Times

If you need to stop for a time which is not on the table. For example, 15 minutes at 46 metres (151 feet) round the time up to the next higher one (in this case 17 minutes) and decompress for this time (five minutes at 10 metres and 10 minutes at five metres).

If you are only doing one dive a day this table provides all the information you need to know. When you surface after your dive, you will still have some nitrogen in solution in your body but this amount should do you no harm and will gradually disappear over the next six hours or so.

Test Questions (answers on page 92)
1. You want to dive to 30 metres (99 feet) without having to do stops. How long can your bottom time be?
2. You intend to dive to 35 metres (115 feet) for 20 minutes. What decompression stops will you have to do on the way back?
3. You want to dive to 36 metres (118 feet) for 20 minutes. What decompression stops will you have to do?

Repeat Dives

Many divers want to dive twice a day to take advantage of the diving conditions and make the most of the opportunities available.

They, therefore, need to have a means of working out what effect the nitrogen still remaining in solution in the body will have on the calculations for the next dive.

This will depend on how long it is since the surfacing from the first dive.

Repeat Dive Tables

The first thing to note is that the second dive will *not* need a stop if it is to a depth of less than nine metres (30 feet).

This is a useful point to remember, particularly when on holiday in a warm water area. It means you can do a 'deep' dive in the morning and then spend as much time as you like in the afternoon in the shallows, as long as you don't go deeper than nine metres.

To make second dives at a greater depth than nine metres, consult the two tables on page 55

Firstly, let's assume that neither of the dives is more than 40 metres (131 feet) a very great depth for beginners.

Diving within 2 hours of First Dive

If you are going to dive again within two hours of surfacing from the first dive, you will have quite a lot of nitrogen still in solution and so will have to count all the bottom time of the first dive as a 'handicap'. You will need to decompress for the time indicated at the deeper of the two dives made.

Sample Calculation

To make it clearer, look at this example:
You dived in the morning to 30 metres (99 feet) for 10 minutes, and, one hour later, intend to dive again to 28 metres (92 feet). The calculation is as follows:
Bottom time of first dive = 10 mins
Time elapsed between dives = 1 hr (less than 2 hours in table)
So, handicap = 10 mins (whole time of first dive)
Planned depth of second dive = 28 m
Deepest dive = 30 m (first dive)
At 30 m there is a 'no stop' time of 20 mins
BUT there is the handicap of 10 mins. Therefore the diver can stay 10 mins (20 mins minus 10 mins) on the second dive without needing a decompression stop.

Diving from 2–4 hours after first dive

If the gap between the two dives is from two to four hours, the handicap is reduced to half the bottom time of the first dive.

Sample Calculation

Taking the same depths and intentions as the first dive the calculation will be:
Bottom time of first dive = 10 mins
Time elapsed = 3 hrs (could be any time between 2 and 4 hours)
Handicap = 5 mins (half time of first dive
Planned depth of next dive = 28 m
Deepest dive = 30 m
No stop time at 30 m = 20 mins
Handicap = 5 mins
Therefore 15 mins (20 minus 5) is the bottom time of the second dive without stops.

Diving 4–6 hours after First Dive

It is usual to have lunch between dives and so it might well be four to six hours after first surfacing that the second dive is made.

The handicap is now only a quarter. Using the same depths and intentions as previously the calculation will be:

Bottom time for first dive = 10 mins
Time elapsed = 4½ hrs
Handicap = 2½ mins
Next dive to 28 m
Deepest dive = 30 m (first dive)
No stop at 30 m = 20 mins
Therefore bottom time for second dive = 17½ mins (20 minus 2½)

If it is over six hours since surfacing you can ignore the first dive and treat the second dive as a first one. Always remember to calculate the decompression time by considering the *deepest* of the two dives *not* just the depth of the dive you are about to make.

Repeat Dive Tables

RNPL/BSAC repeat dive tables deal only with two dives a day. If you do more than this you will have to use other tables; in which case it is strongly advised that the third dive should be shallower than nine metres. You should never stay longer than eight hours in any 24 hour period.

Test Questions (answers on page 92)
1. You have dived to 25 metres (82 feet) in the morning for a bottom time of 20 mins. Two and a half hours after surfacing you are going down again to 20 metres (66 feet). How long can you stay without doing stops?
2. What stops will you need if you stay for 20 mins?

Planning Dives

As a novice you will naturally expect that your instructor or dive leader will plan your dives for you. Unfortunately in some parts of the world this is not always the case. If your dive leader cannot tell you the no-stop time for the depth that he is about to take you to, then you now know how to calculate it yourself.

The person who is planning and leading the dive must have an accurate depth gauge and watch or dive timer. Always take a RNPL/BSAC dive slate to the dive site. Mark the depth and time for your planned dive on the blank side and take the slate with you on the dive.

Finally, be careful about flying too soon after the last dive of your holiday. The rule is do not fly within two hours of surfacing from a no-stop dive or within *24 hours* of surfacing from a dive with stops. Remember too, that you will be just as much at risk if you drive up a mountain following a deep dive.

Divers doing a Decompression Stop

1 The divers monitor their depth and time carefully. When the bottom time is finished, they swim back to their shot line (2).
3 and 4 Divers use the shot line as a guide and ascend, not moving up faster than 15 metres (50 feet) per minute.
5 A spare aqualung is hung on to the shot line at the depth of the stop or stops, in this case at five metres (16½ feet). If the diver gets short of air while waiting at this depth, he can change mouthpieces and breathe from the spare aqualung.
6 On completion of the stop the diver swims slowly up to the cover boat.
7 The cover boat flies a 'Flag A', warning that divers are down.

Nitrogen Narcosis
The increasing amount of nitrogen that divers breath when deep diving can cause other problems which have nothing to do with decompression sickness.

The effects are on the brain and are known as *nitrogen narcosis* or 'the narcs'. They slow down thought processes, cause confusion and general apprehension.

Nitrogen narcosis is somewhat similar to the effects of alcohol and the Americans refer to the increasing effect as 'Martini's Law' (i.e. you react as though you have drunk a martini at each 10 metres or 33 feet during your descent).

In fact, there is usually no great difficulty until you are below 30 metres (99 feet) in cold, murky waters and below 40 metres (131 feet) in clear, warm water. However, everyone reacts differently and young people and others with less resistance may be affected sooner.

If you feel at all dizzy, light-headed or confused during a dive, swim upwards and your head will clear. Fortunately, there are no after effects.

If, however, a diver continues downwards the confusion increases, until he becomes unconscious.

Safety on Deep Dives
Great care should be taken when deep diving. Apart from the planning of the decompression aspects of the dive, a careful programme of introductory dives should be made, each deeper than the one before so that the diver adapts to the target depth.

The confusion or dizziness of nitrogen narcosis is often accompanied by a feeling of apprehension as the diver realises that he is not in complete control of his situation. If he is taken deep too soon, he may be incapable of helping himself.

Divers should check each other carefully during dives when they are going deeper than they have been before. A signal should be agreed that the diver can make if he feels the effects (usually the index finger pointing at the side of the head and moving in circles).

Narcosis can be recognised in your partner by vague and slow replies to signals and by a dreamy look in the eyes. Check him regularly and, if he seems unaware, signal him to rise and, if necessary, help him up to shallower water.

Limits of Diving
Professionals are not allowed to dive deeper than 50 metres (164 feet) on air and this rule should apply to amateur divers too. Deep diving does not make you a better diver, only a diver who is more at risk and most of the interesting marine life is found in shallow water.

You may feel a curiosity to see how you will react to a very deep dive but deep diving is fraught with problems and best avoided.

Right: Symptoms of narcosis vary from individual to individual. If you realise that you are affected, just swim back up and the symptoms will disappear. With experience you will be able to overcome initial effects by concentrating.

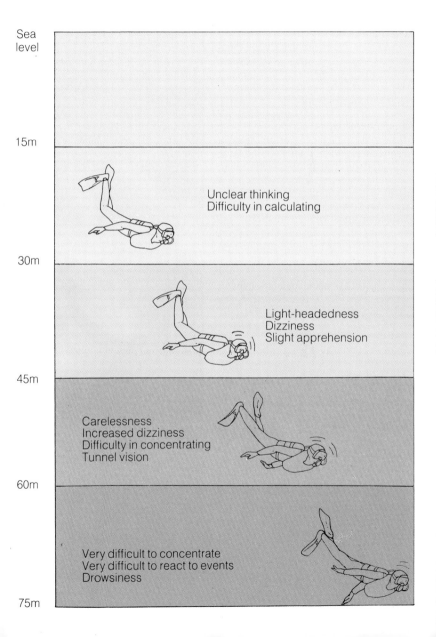

Sea level

15m

Unclear thinking
Difficulty in calculating

30m

Light-headedness
Dizziness
Slight apprehension

45m

Carelessness
Increased dizziness
Difficulty in concentrating
Tunnel vision

60m

Very difficult to concentrate
Very difficult to react to events
Drowsiness

75m

Part 4
The First Dives

The First Dive
When you have finished your pool training and lectures and passed your oral, you are ready for the big day – your first open water dive.

What will it be like?

Your Instructor
One of the most important factors contributing to the success of your first dive will be the person who accompanies you. He should be a calm, caring and qualified instructor who will make seeing *you* enjoy your first dive his priority. The instructor will also ensure that you are not put into situations or depths that you are not ready to cope with.

Everyone feels slightly apprehensive on a first dive and the person who guides you is there to give you help and confidence.

Pre-dive Checks
You will be briefed to check that you remember the hazards of shallow diving – burst lung, mask squeeze, ear clearing and, of course, the signals. Then you will do the pre-dive equipment check. If there is more than one beginner you may be paired-off and will do this with them.

Check that you have your weight belt on, and that your companion does too. Check how his belt quick release works and that it would drop or pull free if you released it in an emergency. Check that you both have your cylinders switched on and that they are not leaking. Check that your direct feeds from demand valve to lifejacket are attached and working. Finally, check that you

have the necessary basic equipment – mask, fins and snorkel with you.

The Dive Plan
Your instructor will explain the dive plan, where you are going, at what depth, and what you may see. He will remind you about adjusting your buoyancy using your direct feed when your suit becomes squeezed by the increasing pressure. He will remind you to stay together but that, if you are separated from the group,

you should surface (after a quick search has been unsuccessful) and reassemble on the surface .

Diving from the Shore

Your first dive should be in calm water and, ideally, from the shore. In British waters, inland dive sites such as Stoney Cove in Leicestershire, provide ideal conditions in which to become accustomed to cold and depth without having to cope with currents and wave conditions.

Above: During expedition dives, a timekeeper keeps an accurate record on the surface. This diver is being helped back on board after a dive to the Etruscan wreck off Giglio.

Getting into the Water

You walk in up to your chest, gradually getting used to the water temperature. Then, on the word from your instructor, you lean forward and breathe out to see if you have enough weight to allow you to sink.

Once he is satisfied you may swim to a line or scaffold pole, down which you begin your descent – probably feet first and clearing your ears gently all the time.

Swimming down a Slope

Alternatively you may just swim down a sloping bottom, adjusting slowly to the increasing depth.

Now for the first time you are aware that you are really under-water, your demand valve hisses and bubbles as you breathe and you may sight your first fish.

If your ears are OK you will gather together on the bottom and check your depth gauge and air supply. You may already feel heavy due to

the air in the suit being squeezed, and you may press your air inlet button to let in a few puffs of air to regain buoyancy.

You take great care to reply promptly to the instructor's *Are you OK?* signal, and try to remember to swim slowly just using your fins.

All too soon the instructor will be giving the 'thumbs up' sign, letting you know that it is time to return to the surface. You swim gently up-wards and let the extra air out from the lifejacket mouthpiece.

Finally, the instructor debriefs you, commenting on the dive and advising you on your technique. You feel that at last you can call yourself a diver!

Below: A First Dive

1 The diver collects all his equipment together and is briefed at the water's edge before (**2**) strapping on the aqualung and doing a 'pre-dive check'.

3 The diver walks backwards in the shallows until the water reaches waist level (**4**).

5 At about chest level, he stops, fits the mask and mouthpiece, leans forward into the water and breathes out to check if he can sink.

6 If ideally weighted, he will remain below the surface, but will not be so heavy that he collides with the bottom. If he is too light, he can return for another weight which is fixed to his weight belt.

7 When the instructor is satisfied, the diver swims with him to the outer edge of the diving platform.

8 He uses the scaffolding as a guide for his descent, sinking feet first and clearing his ears gently with his other hand.

9 After a quick check on the depth and pressure in the cylinders, he answers the instructor's 'Are you OK?' hand signal.

10 He is now ready to follow the instructor down the slope to explore around the wreck. By the time that he reaches it, his suit will have been squeezed slightly making him feel heavier. This is the time to let in a little air through the direct feed to adjust buoyancy.

The First Boat Dive

It may be that your very first dive is from a boat and this is quite acceptable. You will, of course, need to learn further techniques for the boat dive.

In a large boat you will 'kit up' before arriving at the dive site and be briefed and do your 'pre-dive check'. You may let a little air into your lifejacket to give you buoyancy on the surface when you first go in.

If you are diving in tidal waters your dive leader will have a surface marker buoy so that the boat can follow you.

In a small boat, you may kit up completely before leaving if the journey is reasonably short. If it is a long way, you will leave your weight belt and aqualung (demand valve already fitted) off at your feet, ready to put on when you arrive.

Methods of Entry

You should already have practised methods of entry during your pool training. A large dive boat should have a proper fixed ladder set out from the hull so that you can walk up and down it with fins on. If the size of the boat will allow you to stand up safely on the gunwale (the side of the boat), steadying yourself with a stay or on the ladder, then the normal method of entry is to jump.

Step off well clear of the side and enter the water feet first, holding your mask against your face to prevent it being dislodged on impact.

If you are diving from a small boat such as an inflatable dinghy, you will already be sitting on the gunwale facing inwards. When you are

Above: The diver has stepped up on to the gunwale of the boat. After checking that there is no other diver or obstruction below, he holds his mask against his face and jumps outwards, keeping clear of the boat.

Above: The diver leaving from an inflatable boat simply sits in position, facing inwards. When the boat handler has checked that all is ready, the diver rolls backwards holding his mask firmly to his face.

ready, mask in place, you will get the word from the dive leader or cox of the boat and simply roll backwards, holding your mask against your face.

A cloud of bubbles will surround you as you break through the surface and roll over until your lifejacket and fins bring you back to the surface. The first thing to do is to signal to the boat and the dive leader that you are OK.

Making the Descent

Then join up with the leader who will probably be holding on to the SMB at the surface. He will signal for everyone to go down and will sink away unwinding the buoy line. Let the air out of your lifejacket and follow him down his line, trying not to pull on it.

He can see you above him and again will check that you are OK as you stop to clear your ears.

Soon you see the bottom looming below you as though you are 'coming in to land'. The dive leader is waiting for you and you sink to join him and pause while you all check depth gauges and find pressure gauges to make the first check on your air supply.

Below: Diving in Currents and Tides

The safest way to dive in currents and tides. The dive leader holds the reel from which a line ascends to his buoy. He and his companions can drift or swim in any direction while the cover boat follows the buoy on the surface. At the end of the dive, the line is reeled in and the divers return to the buoy and thus to the cover boat.

Following the Dive Leader

It may have been bumpy on the surface but all will be calm at the bottom, although you may already be made aware of a current. When everyone is relaxed and ready, the dive leader indicates the direction and the dive begins. He starts to drift or swim over the bottom with the buoy line curving upwards above him. You follow, not so close that you are brushing his fins and not so far that you will have difficulty in seeing his signals.

You try not to stir up the sand and watch the underwater scenery drift by. You keep one eye on the instructor ahead in case he signals and you adjust your buoyancy when you feel heavy. You 'fly' along, trying to relax as much as possible.

Time Up

After what seems like only a short time, you may notice that your pressure gauge needle is nearly on the red zone. You swim closer to your dive leader and then make the 'clenched fist' signal, showing that you are beginning to run low on air.

The Ascent

He acknowledges with an *OK*, beckons the other divers together and then indicates for you all to go up. You swim gently upwards, sorry to leave this new world behind.

As you rise, you feel your increasing buoyancy as the compressed air expands and you let some out with your direct feed. You keep level with the dive leader who is slowly reeling in the buoy line. He may slow down as the surface appears close above you and may even do a short stop for practice.

At the Surface

Breaking surface, you will be suddenly aware of the waves and that you feel heavy and tired. This is the time to let some air into your life-jacket so that it will support you comfortably on the surface while you wait for the boat to arrive.

You notice the leader making the *OK at surface* signal to the boat.

Getting Back on Board

As the boat approaches you watch carefully to make sure that you are not run down.

If your boat has a dive ladder, grab hold of it with both hands and hook your feet on to the bottom rung.

Coming back on board an inflatable is different. You hang on to the side lines, and, when the cox is ready, you undo your weight belt and pass it up to him. Then detach your direct feed, undo the aqualung waist strap, edge out of one shoulder strap and let him haul your 'lung' on board. When he is ready for you to follow, grip the lines with both hands, bob up and down to gain momentum and then push up, beating your fins until you can get the top half of your body over the side. Then swing yourself round so that you are sitting on the gunwale facing outwards. Finally, you can lift each leg into the boat.

Always remember to keep your more easily damaged gear – mask and depth gauge – close to you in the boat, away from heavy equipment and feet.

Part 5 Holiday Diving

Finding a Good Location

More and more holidaymakers are wanting to learn to dive before they arrive at their holiday dive centre. They are naturally eager to enjoy the undersea world.

The BSAC Novice Diver Programme, although it covers most of the essential information you need to preserve your life underwater, is designed to prepare you for your first open water dives with a *qualified instructor*.

This means that you cannot go to just any dive centre abroad and be able to dive safely. What you need to do is to try and find a holiday location with a *recognised school*.

The main certifying agencies are listed on page 79 and BSAC Schools on page 77.

BSAC Schools will follow the broad outlines of sport diving as outlined in this book and the programme listed on page 80.

Although many Dive Shops and Centres abroad will organise dives, it is important to find one that is being properly led by a qualified instructor for your own safety and enjoyment. Let him know if you have not been in the open sea before.

Some parts of the world have seas that are ideal for beginners – warm, clear and colourful. The West Indies, northern Red Sea, Mediterranean and Indian Ocean are the favourite locations.

Dive Guides

Beware of unqualified 'dive guides' who have been appointed 'off the beach' by hotels. You can assess the capability of such guides by the briefing that they give, or *don't* give you, before a dive.

They should remind you of the hazards – burst lung, mask squeeze, decompression sickness and also check through all the signals they are going to use. They should remind you about ear clearing and how to get back if your air fails.

The pre-dive briefing should also include the depth of the dive that you will be doing, where you will go, what you will see plus any underwater hazards and special instructions (for example: Stay behind and not deeper than the dive leader).

If you are not told the intended depth of the dive, ask, and when you get an answer, ask how long you can stay at this depth without stops on the tables he is using.

Check how you are to be picked up by the boat and when and where if this has not already been made clear. Check you are paired off with someone and then check their experience, finding out if they have shared air before.

Do a pre-dive check. Once on the dive stay with your companion and in sight of the dive leader.

Holiday Hazards

The dangers in British waters are chiefly the cold, low visibility and currents. Equipment and training have been developed to deal with them – efficient suits, compressed air lifejackets, surface marker buoys and powerful inflatables.

The British Isles are surrounded by shallow seas and deep dives usually involve much travelling and advance planning.

The Mediterranean

The Mediterranean Sea is very different. Clear warm water and practically no dangerous sea life. Ideal for beginners except that it is one of the deepest seas. British divers can be unaware of the depth unless they keep a close watch on their depth gauges.

Even in these ideal conditions the problems of deep diving are just as real – narcosis, decompression sickness and high air consumption at depth. Take a decompression slate with you and plan your dives.

Check your air regularly and don't be afraid to come up if you feel 'narcosed'.

There are very few animals that will cause serious harm to a diver. Sea urchins, however, have poisoned spines and should not be touched and neither bristle worms nor scorpion fish should be handled.

The Tropics

Tropical seas are different again. They may be very deep with virtually no shallow area, just a steep 'drop off' down to thousands of feet.

However, on the shallow coral reefs there are vast numbers of resident animals and the sharp coral itself which can give unwary divers very nasty cuts. Most of the stings you can acquire by inadvertently

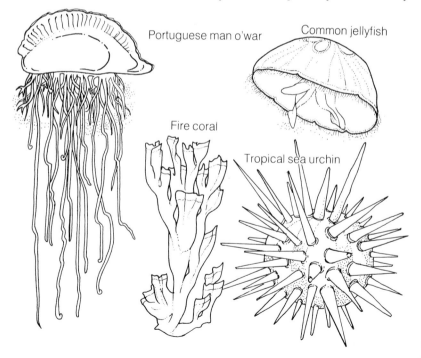

Portuguese man o'war

Common jellyfish

Fire coral

Tropical sea urchin

touching animals are not much more unpleasant than stinging nettles, although a few are deadly.

Most resorts now sell underwater guide books which include lists of creatures that are best avoided.

Fire corals, sponges and hydroids (tiny plant-like animals with stinging cells) grow on reefs and will sting and burn. Fish are generally inoffensive but some, such as the slow-moving and highly coloured lionfish are very poisonous.

Large jellyfish, such as the Portuguese man o' war, can give agonising stings which raise great weals and can send the diver into shock.

Application of alcohol and antihistamine cream will help as will vinegar or lemon juice.

The most deadly organism in the sea is the small tropical sea wasp jellyfish, luckily very rare. Contact with bare skin can cause death.

Wearing a light wet suit on tropical reefs will protect you against many of these creatures. Never wade in shallows without shoes.

Below: Wet suits provide protection against jellyfish stings but some marine animals are extremely dangerous, so be cautious when near unknown species. The stone fish, lionfish and scorpion fish are poisonous as are urchin spines.

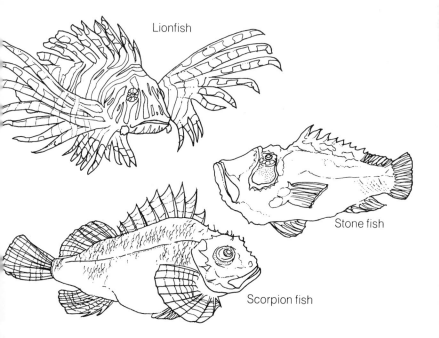

Lionfish

Stone fish

Scorpion fish

Sharks

Sooner or later you will probably come across sharks when diving. They are not as bad as their reputation suggests, although there are always exceptions. The commonest species on dive sites in the tropics are small reef sharks and these are now regularly fed underwater in such places as the Maldive Islands, while holiday divers look on.

A shark is usually very wary of aqualung divers and especially of the strange and frightening bubbles.

If you feel nervous of sharks, stay close to your companion and dive leader when on the bottom.

Hazards from underwater life are dealt with fully in a number of books (see list page 82).

Human Hazards

Humans are usually the most potentially dangerous hazard for a new diver! In the past few years I have seen divers being sent out on their first dives without an instructor, divers being sent on a first night dive without a leader who had been before. I have even given a lecture on decompression to a hotel guide who admitted he 'had never understood it' and who did not possess a watch or timer.

The Golden Rules of Diving are listed on page 76. Try to follow them all the time for your own and other divers' safety.

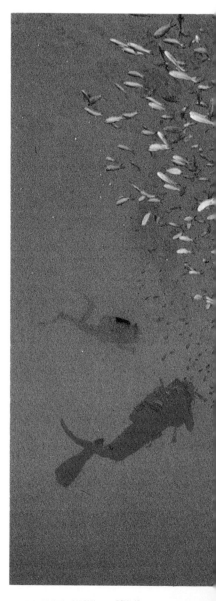

Right: One of the most beautiful holiday dive sites is at Ras Muhammed in the Red Sea. The shoal of pink *Anthias* inhabits the coral reef.

Part 6 Lifesaving and Rescue

The diver operates in an alien environment. If he loses consciousness, he will drop the mouthpiece through which he breathes and, unless help is quickly available, will drown.

Drowning can happen very quickly in fresh water (two minutes) but takes longer in the sea (up to 10 minutes). It is essential therefore that unconscious divers are recovered as quickly as possible and given *expired air resuscitation* (EAR) or the 'kiss of life' to restore their breathing.

Expired Air Resuscitation (EAR)

Check that the victim is not breathing – no movement of chest, blue-grey colour. Then check he has nothing blocking his mouth or throat. Roll him to lie face upwards. Extend the neck by tilting his head right back. If, when he is in this position, a

further check confirms that there is still no sign of breathing, hold the nose shut with the fingers of your left hand while you seal your lips round the victim's and blow sharply into his mouth. His chest should rise as you refill his lungs. After five quick breaths, settle down to blowing at the normal breathing rate. Eventually his colour should improve.

If the subject tries to be sick, roll him on his side so that his mouth and throat can clear and there is no danger of him inhaling vomit.

Once he is breathing, leave him in the coma position (see illustration). Send for medical help if you have not already done so.

Rescue

Accidents may occur at the surface or on the bottom. If something goes wrong on the bottom it will be

LIFESAVING

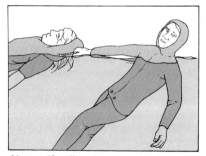

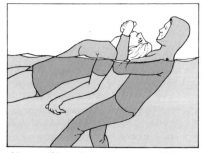

Above: If a diver is relaxed but is exhausted, it may be easiest to tow him or her using this method
The inflated lifejacket will keep the distressed diver's face well clear of the water so he can breathe easily.

Above: If less buoyancy is available, or the distressed diver is semi-conscious, the rescuer holds his head close, keeping it up with his elbow and arm. His air passages are kept open and he can be given E.A.R.

essential to raise the victim.

He may be quite heavy or he may panic and struggle. If he does panic, it will be better to grasp and lift him from behind, but normally a face-to-face position is best, especially with an unconscious diver.

Let air into his lifejacket to help with the lift and, if further buoyancy is needed, remember that you can drop his weight belt. Try not to let too much air into your own jacket in case you lose your grip on him and are parted from him as you rise.

Once you are at the surface you should check his lifejacket is at least partly inflated and take off his mask and mouthpiece to help his breathing. If it has not already been released, take off his weight belt now.

If the victim is still conscious, reassure him that all will be well and signal your boat (waving arm) for immediate assistance.

As a novice diver, it is probably better for you not to try to tow him, unless there is no other option. Some suggested methods of tow are shown in the illustrations below.

Hypothermia

When the water temperature is below 21°C people lose heat very rapidly and, unless divers wear good suits, they may develop hypothermia (extremely low temperature) which results in them becoming very confused and unable to help themselves.

When you are underwater and become cold, always make signals that you want to return.

If a diver becomes very cold, the best action is to wrap him up very warmly and get him to a hot shower or bath and then to bed.

COMA POSITION
Below: When a drowned person has been successfully resuscitated and is breathing normally, he should be put into the 'coma position' until he regains consciousness. If he needs to be transported, he should be kept in this position.

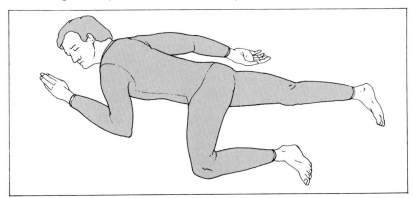

Golden Rules of Diving

If you can relax in the water, always keeping energy in reserve for emergencies, and if you always come back to the surface slowly, you are likely to arrive in good shape.

Basic Rules

1. Never dive alone. Make sure you have a good and qualified instructor with you on your first few dives.
2. Always wear a lifejacket.
3. Always take a SMB in tidal waters or water with currents.
4. Always use a 'direct feed' to adjust your buoyancy.
5. Avoid deep dives and those involving decompression stops unless there is a very good reason for doing them and you have sufficient experience.
6. Plan your dive. Use a diving slate and follow your plan.

Pre-dive Check

1. Check that you have a weight belt on and that it will release. Check your companion's weight belt.
2. Check that you and your dive partner have your air turned on and full cylinders.
3. Check that both your direct feeds are connected.
4. Check that you both have the necessary basic equipment (see page 14).
5. Check that your mask is not too tight.

On the Dive

1. Check your weight in the shallows if using a new suit. Never take more weight than you need.
2. Practice mask clearing and sharing in the shallows if you are out of practice.
3. Never 'force' your ears to clear. Always come up slightly and blow *gently* through your closed-off nose. Ears are delicate.
4. Always stay together.
5. If your mask 'sucks' on to your face, blow more air into it from your nose.
6. Don't try to lift heavy objects without the right equipment to do so.
7. Don't interfere with other underwater inhabitants.
8. If you feel the effects of narcosis, swim up to shallower depths. Check that your companion is replying to your signals. Help *him* up if necessary.
9. Never hold your breath when coming up. If you have to surface alone and without air, breathe out steadily on the way up.

Remember that the best diver is not the one who makes the deepest dives – the best diver is the one who always comes back safely!

British Sub-Aqua Club Schools

If you want to learn to dive as quickly as possible, the BSAC recommends that you use one of the diving schools that are recognized by them. These schools are staffed by nationally qualified instructors and are inspected by the governing body. They run introductory courses, novice diver courses and sport diver courses.

The *Introductory Course* gives the opportunity to try the sport in a safe pool. The *Novice Diver Course* qualifies you to dive in open water with a qualified instructor. Techniques are taught in pools and lectures are also given during these sessions. The *Sports Diver Course* takes you into open water and qualifies you to dive with any other diver, providing that diver is not a trainee. The course includes ten open water dives in varying conditions and lectures and drills.

Many schools also run their own BSAC branches which can award higher qualifications.

Schools may offer full-time courses, evening and day classes and private tuition. Contact individual schools for further information.

BSAC Schools in England

London Underwater Centre
13 Glendower Road
London SW14 8NY
Tel: 01-876 0735

Fort Bovisand Underwater Centre
Plymouth
Devon, PL9 OAB
Tel: 0752 48021

Divers Down Diving School
The Pier
Swanage, Dorset BH19 2AN
Tel: 092942 3565

Exeter Diving Services
Belmont Road
Exeter, Devon
Tel: 0392 59439

Aquasport International
80 Alcester Road
Molesey, Birmingham B13 8BB
Tel: 021 449 2572/4148

Diver Training School
The Quayside,
Exmouth Harbour, Devon
Tel: 03952 6300

Aquaticus Diving School
101 Huddersfield Road
Oldham, Lancs OL1 3NQ
Tel: 061 665 1370

North Western Watersports
2 Salford Road
Over Hulton
Bolton, Lancs, BL5 1BL
Tel: 0204 652212

Cornish Diving Services
Bar Road
Falmouth, Cornwall
Tel: 0326 311265

Stoney Cove Diver Training
Stoney Cove
Stoney Stanton, Leics LE9 6DW
Tel: 045 527 3089

Ocean Marine Technical Services
Sanderson Centre
Gosport, Hants PO12 3UL
Tel: 0705 529843

Comdean Scuba Training Centre
68 Stratford Road, Shirley
Solihull, W. Midlands B90 3LP
Tel: 021 744 1526

Truro Diving Services
38 Lemon Street
Truro, Cornwall
Tel: 0872 77652/70742

Fylde Coast Diving Centre
40 Cookson Street
Blackpool, Lancs FY1 3ED
Tel: 0253 293245

The Poole Dive Centre
2 Merryfield Lane
Kinson, Dorset BH10 5HN
Tel: 0202 577190

The Dive Centre
5 Middleton
Bretton, Peterborough PE3 6XQ
Tel: 0733 268949

BSAC Schools in Wales
Anglesey Diving & Watersports
Garden Cottage, Soldiers Point
Holyhead, Anglesey LL65 1YF
Tel: 0407 50440

Treasure Island Diving Services
Old Promenade
Aberavon Beach
Port Talbot, W Glamorgan
Tel: 0639 884108

BSAC Schools in Scotland
Strathclyde Diving School
3 Houston Place
Glasgow G5 8SG
Tel: 041 429 5902

Under C Diving School
8 Maxwell Road
Bishopton, Renfrewshire PA7 5HE
Tel: 050 586 2449

BSAC Schools Overseas
Divewise Services Limited
Dragonara Watersports Centre
Dragonara Hotel
St Julians, Malta
Tel: Malta 36441

Maltaqua
Mosta Road
St Paul's Bay, Malta
Tel: Malta 571873

Cydive Limited
1 Poseidon Avenue
Kato Paphos, Cyprus
Tel: Cyprus (061) 34271

Eden Rock Diving Center
PO Box 1907
Grand Cayman
Cayman Islands, BWI
Tel: (809 949) 7243

Marine Sports
Marina Bay Yacht Agency
3 Admirals Walk, Marina Bay
PO Box 80, Gibraltar
Tel: Gibraltar 76411

BSAC Novice and Sports Diver Courses

Novice Diver

The BSAC *Novice Diver* qualification was introduced in 1985 to replace the previous BSAC standards of **E** and **F** or 'Elementary/Sports' Certificates.

The World Underwater Federation (CMAS) recognises this standard as CMAS One Star Diver. Certificates are available from BSAC headquarters.

The Novice Diver course includes lectures on: introduction to training, basic equipment, signals, causes and effects of pressure, aqualung breathing apparatus, human life support system, buoyancy devices, diver rescue, safe diving practice, diving suits and accessories, equipment care and storage, dry suit diving and where to dive. The lectures are followed by a theory test.

Practical sessions are given covering use of mask, fins and snorkel, aqualung, breath-holding diving, ABLJ/BC skills, rescue skills, and full equipment familiarization.

Sport Diver

The BSAC *Sport Diver* Standard was introduced to replace 'Third Class Diver' standard. The Sport Diver has gained a variety of open water diving experience and is ready to dive with another diver of the same, or higher, standard. He will *not* be expected to dive with Novice Divers. The World Underwater Federation (CMAS) recognises this standard as *CMAS Two Star Diver*.

The Sports Diver course includes lectures on diver rescue, diving from boats, underwater navigation, nitrogen absorption and gas toxicity, deep diving, decompression tables, air requirements, organizing dives and safety. It is followed by a theory test.

Practical sessions cover rescue skills, underwater navigation, use of SMBs and a safety and rescue skills test. Ten open water dives will have been completed at five different locations, on five different dates and giving experience of five different conditions chosen from the following: shore dive, small boat dive, fresh water dive, current dive (one knot), sea dive, low visibility dive (two metres), cold dive ($10°C$) and deep dive (25 metres).

Further Qualifications

Following these qualifications, divers may qualify as *Dive Leaders*.

Later they may qualify as *Advanced Divers* whose experience is tested and recognised and which allows them .to lead and organize diving activities within a branch of BSAC. The World Underwater Federation recognises this as a *CMAS Three Star Diver* standard.

First Class Divers (*CMAS Four Star Diver*) are qualified on a nationally organised examination and may lead projects or expeditions.

BSAC Instructors

There are three grades of BSAC instructors, all of whom are qualified on a national examination:

1. *BSAC Club Instructor* (*CMAS One Star Instructor*). 2. *BSAC Advanced Instructor* (*CMAS Two Star Instructor*). 3. *BSAC National Instructor* (*CMAS Three Star Instructor*).

Useful Addresses

UK

BSAC

The British Sub-Aqua Club
16 Upper Woburn Place
London WC1H 0QW
Tel: 01-387 9302

The BSAC is the UK Governing Body of the sport with over 1,000 branches world-wide. Its standards are accepted by the World Underwater Federation (CMAS) for the issue of international certificates and cards. Members receive a copy of the *BSAC Diving Manual* and monthly copies of the magazine *Diver*. Lists of branches are available from the above address.

SAA

The Sub-Aqua Association
Ocean Publications
22/24 Buckingham Palace Road
London SW1 0QP
Tel: 01-828 4551

The SAA bands independent clubs together in the UK. It has some 400 member clubs.

NSC

National Snorkellers Club
13 Langham Gardens
Wembley, Middx HA0 3RG

The NSC caters for juniors who are not old enough to use aqualungs. Run by Lionel Blandford, it has hundreds of branches throughout the country where youngsters learn to use mask, fins and snorkel tube and qualify for a range of awards. The NSC also run holiday courses abroad.

BSAC Schools

The Association of BSAC Recognised Schools
16 Upper Woburn Place
London WC1H 0QW
Tel: 01-387 9302

The Association includes those schools with nationally or internationally qualified instructors (see pages 77–78).

PASS

Professional Association of SCUBA Schools
19 Point Terrace
Exmouth, Devon EX8 1EF
Tel: 0395 266300

An independent organisation of diving schools.

BSoUP

British Society of Underwater Photographers
c/o BSAC (address above).

BSoUP provides a forum for keen underwater photographers, organises regular meetings and publishes a data book.

NAS

Nautical Archaeology Society
Mem. Sec. Ms V Fenwick
1 The Old Hall
Highgate, London N6 6BP

NAS exists for those interested in underwater archaeology. A journal and newsletter are sent to members and meetings arranged.

MCS

Marine Conservation Society
Dr Bob Earll
4 Gloucester Road
Ross-on-Wye, Herefordshire.

MCS organises surveys and projects for divers interested in conservation.

USA
PADI
Professional Association of Diving Instructors
1243 East Warner Avenue
Box 15550, Santa Ana
Calif. 92705 USA
PADI is the largest American 'certifying' agency which provides publications and course programmes which are followed by many thousands of instructors and divers. There are PADI instructors operating in many countries.

NAUI
National Association of Underwater Instructors
PO Box 630
Colton, Calif. 92324, USA
NAUI also certifies instructors and has a range of publications and courses. NAUI is a member of CMAS and organizes an International Conference of Underwater Education (IQ) each year.

YMCA SCUBA
National YMCA SCUBA Headquarters
1611 Candler Building
Atlanta, Georgia 30303, USA.
YMCA SCUBA also provide SCUBA courses and standards using their swimming pool facilities.

International
CMAS
The World Underwater Federation
34 rue du Colisée
75008 Paris, France
CMAS has national diving federations as its members and is the only international body. General Assemblies are organized every two years and competitions, technical matters and scientific work are covered. The CMAS issues international certificates to those with a recognized national certificate.

UMS
The Undersea Medical Society
9650 Rockville Pike
Bathesda
Maryland 20014, USA
Full UMS members are doctors with an interest in diving medicine. A newsletter, *Pressure*, and a journal are produced by the Society.

Magazines

UK
Diver
40 Grays Inn Road
London WC1X 8LR

Subaqua Scene
Ocean Publications
22/24 Buckingham Palace Road
London SW1 0QP

USA
Skindiver
Petersen Publishing Company
8490 Sunset Blvd
Los Angeles, Calif 90069, USA

Ocean Realm
2333 Brickell Ave
Miami, Florida 33129, USA

Scuba Times
PO Box 6268
Pensacola
Florida 32503, USA

Books

BSAC Diving Manual
obtainable from BSAC, 16 Upper Woburn Place, London WC1H 0QW.
A comprehensive guide to the techniques of underwater swimming.

Divers and Diving
by Reg Vallintine (Blandford 1981).
The background and history of sport, military and commercial diving.

Dangerous Marine Animals
by Bruce Halstead MD (Cornell Maritime Press 1980).
Comprehensive handbook of sea creatures that bite, sting, shock or are non-edible together with suggested treatment.

The Hamlyn Guide to the Seashore and Shallow Seas of Britain and Europe
by AC Campbell (Hamlyn 1976)
Illustrated colour guide to sea life.

Marine Life
by W de Haas and F. Knorr (Burke)
Another guide to the sea life of northern European and Mediterranean waters.

Glossary

'A' clamp Portion of demand valve which allows it to be attached to the cylinder.

'A' flag Flag from the International Code of Signals meaning *Diver down, keep clear.*

ABLJ Adjustable buoyancy lifejacket, using compressed air.

Air consumption Amount or rate of air used by aqualung diver.

Air embolism Kind of burst lung accident in which bubbles of air enter the blood stream.

Alveoli Tiny membranes surrounding the lungs through which gases diffuse when breathing.

Aqualung British name for compressed air breathing apparatus used by sports divers. Known as SCUBA in America.

Backpak Moulded plastic support for aqualung forming part of harness.

Ballooning Rising out of control, usually as a result of expanding compressed air in the diver's suit or lifejacket.

Basic equipment Mask, fins and snorkel tube.

BC Buoyancy compensator. Type of American lifejacket.

Bends Traditional name for decompression sickness.

Blob buoy Surface marker buoy.

Bootees Portion of diving suit that covers the feet and ankles.

Bottom time The time from leaving the surface until leaving the bottom to return to the surface.

Bounce dive Rapid dive to bottom for a short duration.

Boyle's Law Law formulated by Robert Boyle governing relation between pressure and volume of a gas.

Buddy breathing Technique in which two divers share one mouthpiece.

Buoyant ascent Emergency return to the surface after inflating a compressed air lifejacket.

Burst lung Serious condition caused by an aqualung diver holding his breath while ascending.

Compressor Machine used to fill cylinders with air. Diving compressors work to high pressures and include filters to ensure pure air.

Console Unit which includes pressure gauge and other gauges such as depth gauge, timer or compass.

Contents gauge See Pressure gauge.

Cylinder Steel or aluminium container for high pressure air breathed by the diver. Commonly known as a 'bottle' in the UK and as a 'tank' in the USA.

Cylinder capacity Amount of air held by a cylinder. Depends on size of cylinder and pressure to which it is filled.

Decompression dive Dive which involves the diver in decompression stops.

Decompression meter Device to automatically indicate decompression stops that are needed.

Decompression sickness Condition caused by dissolved nitrogen usually appearing as bubbles in the blood and tissues during a too rapid ascent.

Decompression stops Pauses made by the diver close to the surface to avoid decompression sickness. Calculated by using decompression tables.

Decompression tables Method of calculating how and when to return to the surface to avoid decompression sickness.

Demand valve Valve which automatically reduces the diver's air pressure to that of the surrounding water.

Depth gauge Device indicating the diver's depth beneath the surface.

Direct feed Pressure tube that allows air to be passed from the demand valve into the diver's lifejacket.

Ditch and retrieve Technique of removing and replacing equipment.

Dive centre Commercial base for sport diving usually arranging dives and dive boats and having a dive shop and lecture room.

Dive guide Professional guide who leads divers in the water at holiday locations. Dive guides are not necessarily instructors.

Dive leader Person in charge of another, or small group, underwater.

Dive timer Device that automatically registers the time since the diver left the surface.

Drift diving Dive on which the divers drift along the bottom with the prevailing current.

Dry suit Diving suit that keeps the diver dry and protected in very cold conditions.

Duck dive Sequence of actions that are often used to go down from the surface. Entails lying still then bending downwards from the waist and swinging legs out of the water.

Dump valve Valve on ABLJ that releases air quickly to slow down an ascent.

Duration Time from leaving surface to returning to surface.

EAR Expired Air Resuscitation. The method of breathing air into a person whose breathing has stopped. From mouth to mouth or mouth to nose.

Ear clearing Action taken by a diver during descent resulting in increased air pressure in the middle ear.

Equalizing Ear clearing on descent.

Eustachian tube Tube connecting the middle ear with the throat and enabling ears to be cleared during descent.

Fins or flippers Rubber extensions of the foot which, when beaten as in a crawl stroke, push the diver forward.

First stage Part of demand valve that reduces air pressure to approximately 10 atmospheres above ambient or surrounding pressure.

Free ascent Emergency swimming ascent to the surface by an aqualung diver.

Gunwale Raised extension of a boat's hull surrounding the deck and which divers use to jump or roll backwards from when entering the sea.

HP High pressure. As in 'HP hose'.

Harness System of straps that attach an aqualung to the diver's back. Usually consists of two shoulder straps, backpak and waist belt.

Helmet diving Traditional form of commercial diving in which the diver wears a metal helmet attached to a suit. Air is pumped down to him from the surface.

Hypothermia Condition of inertia caused by cold.

Inflatable Rubber inflatable dinghy used by many divers. Should have a powerful and efficient motor and crew.

'In the red' Needle of pressure gauge in the red or low pressure area on the dial and indicating need to return to the surface.

Lifejacket Buoyancy aid worn by diver.

Lock Part of recompression chamber which can be pressurized separately to allow a visitor to enter.

Long john Diving suit trousers that incorporate an attached vest.

Mask Glass face plate in rubber moulding which enables the diver to see clearly underwater. Should include the nose inside.

Mask clearing Exercise of blowing water out of the mask.

Mask squeeze Uncomfortable mask pressure caused by lack of air inside. Cured by blowing out through the nose.

Membrane dry suit Dry suit made of thin rubber material and fitted with valves to adjust buoyancy.

Mouthpiece Portion of snorkel or demand valve through which the diver breathes.

Pillar valve Valve at top of cylinder which includes a tap to switch on the air.

Pony rig Separate small reserve cylinder for use in emergency.

Pre-dive check A check that all essential equipment is present and functioning before entering the water.

Pressure gauge Dial attached to high pressure hose and fixed to the demand valve. Indicates air pressure in the cylinder. Sometimes called a contents gauge.

Narcs *See* Nitrogen narcosis.

Neoprene Springy material from which many diving suits are made.

Nitrogen narcosis Effect of nitrogen on the brain when deep diving. Causes confusion and other symptoms.

No stop dive Dive that does not involve decompression stops.

No stop time Time which a diver can stop at a given depth and still return to the surface without decompression stops.

'O' ring Ring-shaped washer that lies in a groove against the pillar valve to allow an airproof seal to be made with the demand valve.

Octopus rig Extra mouthpiece connected to a demand valve for use by another diver suffering air failure.

Purge valve Portion at front of second stage of demand valve that can be pressed to get extra air or to expel water from the mouthpiece.

Quick release System that allows equipment to be taken off quickly in emergency.

Recompression chamber Pressure vessel in which a diver is recompressed in air to relieve symptoms of burst lung or decompression sickness.

Regulator American term for demand valve.

Repeat dive Dive undertaken while diver still has dissolved nitrogen in the blood from a previous dive.

Reserve System of air reserve which should be sufficient to allow the diver to regain the surface.

SCUBA Self-contained underwater breathing apparatus.

Second stage Part of demand valve including a mouthpiece which reduces air pressure to that of the surrounding water.

Sharing Technique in which two divers share one mouthpiece.

Shorty suit One-piece jacket, usually with short sleeves, and short trousers used in tropical diving.

Shot line Line with buoy at one end and anchor or weight at other forming a vertical marker for an object on the sea bed and providing a means for divers to descend and ascend.

Silicone mask Dive mask made of long-lasting translucent silicone rubber.

Slate Diver's writing slate, often backed with a decompression table.

SLJ Surface lifejacket. Not equipped with compressed air attachments.

SMB Surface marker buoy. Used by divers to mark their position when diving in currents.

Snorkelling Term generally used for the sport of breath-hold diving using a mask, fins and snorkel tube. Also known as snorkel diving.

Snorkel tube Short tube with mouthpiece used for breathing at the surface. Prevents the diver having to lift his head out of the water to breathe.

Squeeze Effect felt by aqualung divers when air inside the suit is insufficient to resist the water pressure.

Stab jacket Kind of compressed air lifejacket giving stability and lift and attached as part of the aqualung.

Staggers and shakes Traditional terms for serious decompression sickness symptoms.

Sticky ears Difficulty experienced in clearing ears on descent.

Where to Dive

Surfacing End part of dive entailing divers swimming back up to the surface.

Tank American term for diving cylinder.

Tank boot Protective heavy rubber base which allows cylinder to stand on end.

Test certificate Certificate showing that aqualung cylinder has been pressure tested and found satisfactory.

Weight belt Belt with lead weights and quick release buckle to adjust the diver's buoyancy.

Wet suit Traditional sport diver's suit that is not completely water-proof but gives warmth and protection and is easy to use.

Woolly bear Warm undersuit for use under dry suits.

In the early days of sport diving, divers tended to dive only in their local waters. This has long since changed. Large and small expeditions are organised by BSAC – both on a national basis and by branches and clubs.

Above all, millions of people go on holiday to places where the sun is hot and the sea is warm and clear. As a diver, you may well find a dive centre nearby. Why not try a dive with them?

Alternatively, you may want to have a whole diving holiday. Whichever way you do it, you are adding another dimension to your holiday.

Sub-tropical Diving
The Mediterranean
For European divers, the easiest and least expensive dive holidays and centres are on the Mediterranean.

Spain has been one of the most popular holiday locations, but diving regulations there, both for visitors and local divers, have tended to inhibit diving development. Nevertheless there are popular centres, particularly in the Balearics. Such centres may be able to get the necessary permits for you, but you should check this with the BSAC Holiday Information Service (Information Officer, Fred Lock, Tel: 036 32 3048).

France has many centres on the Mediterranean coast and some highly organized diving schools.

Italy provides diving shops and compressors at many dive sites. However, divers may find that the extensive spearfishing has reduced

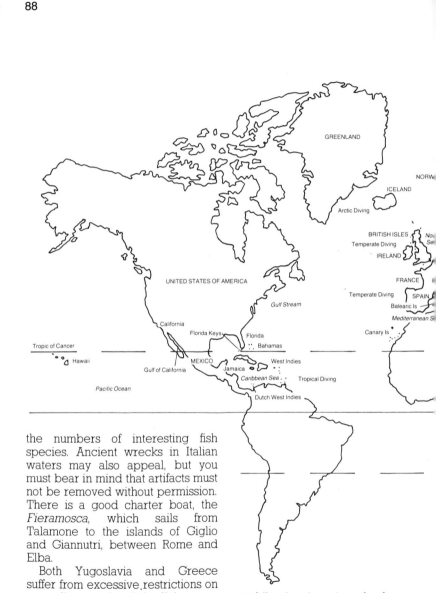

the numbers of interesting fish species. Ancient wrecks in Italian waters may also appeal, but you must bear in mind that artifacts must not be removed without permission. There is a good charter boat, the *Fieramosca*, which sails from Talamone to the islands of Giglio and Giannutri, between Rome and Elba.

Both Yugoslavia and Greece suffer from excessive restrictions on sport divers and so little diving tourism is organized. If you wish to dive always check beforehand, particularly if planning to visit Greece.

The North African coast is only patchily developed so far but can provide really excellent diving.

The islands of Cyprus and Malta both provide excellent diving facilities, including BSAC schools (see

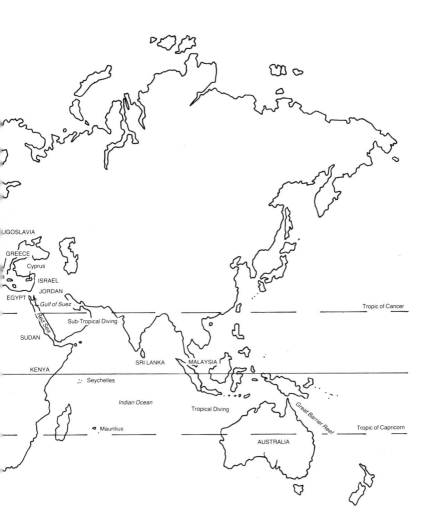

The following labels appear on the map:

YUGOSLAVIA

GREECE

Cyprus

ISRAEL

JORDAN

EGYPT

Gulf of Suez

Red Sea

Sub-Tropical Diving

SUDAN

KENYA

SRI LANKA

MALAYSIA

Seychelles

Indian Ocean

Tropical Diving

Great Barrier Reef

Tropic of Cancer

Tropic of Capricorn

Mauritius

AUSTRALIA

pages 77–78).

The Canaries

The Atlantic Canary Islands have dive centres on a number of islands, many are run by German organizations, the Germans being the most numerous diving tourists in Europe.

A very good 'club' is organised on Lanzarote by an ex-Royal Navy Petty Officer, Bob Wright, and diving is just beginning to be organised on the island of Fuerteventura.

Tropical Diving
The Red Sea
The 'Mecca' for European tropical divers is the Red Sea. It represents not only the nearest tropical waters, but has some of the most luxuriant coral reefs in the world. Few divers can ever return feeling dissatisfied with diving in the Red Sea – although many may be less pleased with what exists, or does not exist, above the surface!

Israel is well provided with centres on its short Red Sea coast, most diving is centred on Eilat. The best known organization is *Aquasport* on the beach at Eilat, originally create by Willy Hapert.

On the other side of the Gulf of Aqaba in Jordan, diving tourism is increasing; Bunny Colclough from England arranges the diving at the *Aquamarina Hotel Club* and Carlos Schaak of Germany runs the *Barakuda Club*.

In Egypt's Gulf of Suez, the small town of Hurghada houses a large centre run by Rudi Kneip, a German who houses divers in primitive local houses and provides large dive boats to the best diving areas.

Further south in Egypt, at Safaga, there is a hotel dive centre. Also two really excellent British registered and crewed dive boats, the *Lady Jenny V*, and *Lady Jenny III*, charter out of Sharm el Sheikh and provide luxurious transport to some of the best Red Sea diving.

Yet further south, in Sudanese waters, a dive centre exists on a coral reef off the coast. Conditions are primitive but the diving can be exhilarating with manta rays, sharks and some beautiful wrecks.

The Indian Ocean
Further east in the Indian Ocean lie some of the most beautiful islands on earth.

The Seychelles, Mauritius and the Maldive Islands are all well-known for their diving facilities.

The Maldives consist of over 1500 tiny islands – coral atolls – many of which have attractive bungalow hotels amid tropical vegetation.

Sri Lanka has a number of centres, too, and the best diving is generally considered to be at Hikkaduwa in the south, although this may depend on the prevailing monsoon. To the west of the Indian Ocean, Kenya also provides excellent diving facilities along with an underwater reserve.

South-East Asia
Sport diving is now developing in Malaysia and Sulawesi. The island of Palau east of the Philippines is said to have more species of coral than any other area in the world.

Australia
Further south again lies the Great Barrier Reef of Australia, another 'Mecca' for the travelled diver – the largest coral reef in the world. The best diving here is off the outer reefs and boats are organised from coastal towns and from the 'Sunshine Coast'. There is a centre at Heron Island at the southern tip of the reef.

Florida, Bahamas and Caribbean
Flying westwards from Europe, it is

only a few hours to Miami, the jumping off place for the Florida Keys which, together with the Bahamas are excellent places for beginners as they have fairly shallow, clear waters. More experienced divers may prefer the excitement of diving offshore in the Gulf Stream to the north, and West Palm Beach is the centre for this. You can also explore the tranquil Crystal River on Florida's west coast and dive with the harmless sea cows, the manatees.

The Caribbean islands are probably the most developed holiday diving regions in the world with hótel centres on many islands. Facilities here are usually excellent but can be expensive.

Many islands advertise their diving potential and the Cayman Islands, west of Jamaica, have specialised in diving. Bonaire, in the Dutch West Indies, is another highly recommended island.

On the Caribbean coast of Mexico the best diving is probably provided at Cozumel Island.

The Pacific Ocean
On Mexico's Pacific Coast there is cooler water diving in the Gulf of California, a tremendously exciting dive area with sea lions and mantas.

Allegedly the best diving area in the world are the Cocos Islands, in the Pacific Ocean off Panama.

The Pacific islands will be one of the biggest diving areas in the future. Already Hawaii is popular and the little island of Truk in Micronesia has become famous for visitors who dive to the wrecks of the sunken Japanese fleet.

Holiday diving preferences vary from diver to diver and there are now so many opportunities that it is impossible to mention them all. Some organisations such as the French *Club Mediterranée* have schools in their 'villages' in many parts of the world.

Temperate and Arctic Diving
Diving in the cold north or extreme south of the world can be very different and the word 'expedition' is more often used. The BSAC Expeditions Section with its indefatigable organizer, Gordon Ridley, run regular voyages in motor fishing boats to the Outer Hebrides of Scotland and to Norway, Iceland and, it is planned, Greenland. You may be lucky enough to see killer whales and will almost certainly dive with seals.

The British Isles
Last, but not least, the British Isles can provide fascinating diving with wrecks (arguably more than anywhere else in the world) seals, basking sharks and cold water corals.

Divers tend to move away from the murky English Channel and North Sea to South West England, Wales and the Scottish Islands. There are excellent diving centres on Lundy Island (in the Bristol Channel), the Scillies, the Isle of Man, Anglesey and in South West Ireland. All seas and waters have their own fascination both above and below the surface.

Holiday Organisations
BSAC Holiday Information Service
9 Tower Gardens
Crediton, Devon

Fieramosca Cruises
13 Glendower Road
London SW14 8NY

Clubulanza (Lanzarote)
Springfield Road
Horsham, W. Sussex RH12 2PJ

Jasmin Tours Ltd (Jordan)
High Street
Cookham, Maidenhead
Berks SL6 9SQ

Red Sea Aquarians (Hurghada)
Hill House
94 Foxley Lane, Purley
Surrey CR2 3NA

Underwater Safaris Ltd
25 Barnes Place
Colombo 7, Sri Lanka

Twickers World
(*Lady Jenny Charters*)
22 Church Street
Twickenham, Middx TW1 3NW

Twickenham Travel
84 Hampton Road
Twickenham, Middx TW2 5QS

Divers World Holidays Ltd
37 Victoria Road
Surbiton
Surrey KT6 4JL

Explorers Sudan
2 Mount Close
Woking, Surrey GU22 0PZ

Club Mediterranée
106–108 Brompton Road
London SW3 1JJ

BSAC Expeditions
c/o Gordon Ridley
94 Brownside Road
Cambuslang
Glasgow G72 8AG

Aquaserve Diving (Lundy Island)
221 Percy Road
Whitton, Middx TW2 6JL

Test Question Answers

Page 56
1. 20 minutes

2. 5 minutes at 10 metres and
   5 minutes at 5 metres.

3. 5 minutes at 10 metres and
   5 minutes at 5 metres.

Page 58
1. You have a 10-minute 'handicap'
   from the first dive.
   Deepest dive level – 25 metres.
   Therefore 27 minutes less 10
   minutes = 17 minutes.

2. 10 minutes handicap
   25 metres = deepest dive
   32 minutes less 10 = 22 minutes
   possibility.
   Stops will be: 5 minutes at 10
   metres and 5 minutes at 5 metres.

Index